Educational Assessment on Trial

Educational Assessment on Trial

ANDREW DAVIS AND CHRIS WINCH

EDITED BY GERARD LUM

Bloomsbury Academic
An imprint of Bloomsbury Publishing Plc

B L O O M S B U R Y
LONDON · NEW DELHI · NEW YORK · SYDNEY

Bloomsbury Academic

An imprint of Bloomsbury Publishing Plc

50 Bedford Square
London
WC1B 3DP
UK

1385 Broadway
New York
NY 10018
USA

www.bloomsbury.com

British Library Cataloguing-in-Publication Data
A catalogue record for this book is available from the British Library.

ISBN: PB: 978-1-4725-7229-5
ePDF: 978-1-4725-7231-8
ePub: 978-1-4725-7230-1

Library of Congress Cataloging-in-Publication Data
A catalog record for this book is available from the Library of Congress.

Series: Key Debates in Educational Policy

Typeset by Integra Software Services Pvt. Ltd
Printed and bound in Great Britain

Contents

Afterword: Can the Two Positions be Reconciled?

Gerard Lum 107

Series Editor's Preface

IMPACT pamphlets were launched in 1999 as an initiative of the Philosophy of Education Society of Great Britain. Their aim was to bring philosophical perspectives to bear on UK education policy and they have been written by leading general philosophers or philosophers of education. There are now more than twenty volumes.

They dealt with a variety of issues relating to policy within the field of education. Some have focused on controversial aspects of current government policy such as those by Andrew Davis on assessment, Harry Brighouse on disparities in secondary education, Mary Warnock on changes in provision for pupils with special educational needs and Colin Richards on school inspection. Others, such as those by Michael Luntley on performance-related pay and by Chris Winch on vocational education and training, have been critical of new policy initiatives. Yet, others have been concerned with the organization and content of the school curriculum. These have included pamphlets by Kevin Williams on the teaching of foreign languages, Steve Bramall and John White on Curriculum 2000, David Archard on sex education, Stephen Johnson on thinking skills, Graham Haydon on personal, social and health education, and John Gingell on the visual arts.

The launch of each pamphlet was accompanied by a symposium for policy makers and others at which issues raised in the pamphlets have been further explored. These have been attended by government ministers, opposition spokespersons, other MPs, representatives from the Qualifications and Curriculum Authority, employers' organizations, trades unions and teachers' professional organizations, as well as members of think tanks, academics and journalists.

Some of the original pamphlets have made a lasting impression on the world of education policy and have, in addition, sparked debates in both the policy and academic worlds. They have revealed a hunger for dealing with certain topics in a philosophically oriented way, because it has been felt that the original pamphlet initiated a debate that needs and deserves to be taken a lot further. The Key Debates in Educational Policy series aimed to take some of these debates further by selecting from those original Impact pamphlets whose influence continues to be keenly felt and either reproducing or expanding them to take account of the most recent developments in the area with which they deal. In addition, each of the original pamphlets receives a lengthy reply by a distinguished figure in the area who takes issue with the main arguments of the original pamphlet. Each of the Key Debates volumes also contained a substantial foreword and afterword by an academic with strong interests in the area under discussion, which gave the context and provided extensive commentary on the questions under discussion and the arguments of the original author and his or her respondent.

There are a number of reasons for this. Philosophical techniques applied to policy issues can be very powerful tool clarifying questions and developing arguments based on ethical, aesthetic, political and epistemological positions. Philosophical argumentation is, however, by its nature, controversial and contested. There is rarely, if ever, one side to a philosophical question. The fact that the Impact pamphlets have often aroused lively debate and controversy is testament to this. There has been a hunger for a more rounded version of the debate to be presented in a format accessible to those who do not have a formal philosophical background, but who find philosophical argumentation about educational issues to be useful in developing their own ideas. This series aimed to cater for this audience while also presenting rigorous argumentation that can also appeal to a more specialist audience.

It was hoped that each volume in this series would provide an introduction and set the scene to each topic and give the readership a splendid example of philosophical argumentation over a complex and important educational issue.

Notes on Contributors

Andrew Davis is Honorary Research Fellow at Durham University, UK. He taught in primary schools for many years before lecturing at Cambridge University, UK, in philosophy of education and maths education, and moving on to Durham University, UK, to teach and research similar topics. His extensive publications about educational assessment include *The Limits of Educational Assessment* (1998). In 2014, his short book *To Read or Not to Read: Decoding Synthetic Phonics* provoked widespread controversy.

Christopher Winch is Professor of Educational Philosophy and Policy at King's College London, UK, where he served as Head of Department from 2008 to 2012. He was Chairman of the Philosophy of Education Society of Great Britain (PESGB) from 2008 to 2011 and Editor of the Impact policy pamphlet series for the PESGB for several years. He has worked in primary, further and higher education and is the author of numerous books and articles on topics in the philosophy of education, vocational and professional education and sociolinguistics. He is the author of *Dimensions of Expertise* (2010) and *Teacher's Knowledge and Know-how* (forthcoming).

Gerard Lum is Lecturer in Philosophy and Education Management in the Department of Education and Professional Studies at King's College London, UK. With extensive experience of assessment design in vocational and professional education, his current research interests are centred on problems relating to knowledge and assessment. He has published widely on topics in philosophy of education, and his book *Professional and Vocational Capability: An Epistemological and Ontological Study of Occupational Expertise* was published in 2009.

Introduction

Gerard Lum

This book is about the contentious issue of the place of assessment in education. There are two related reasons why this issue has come to particular prominence now, at this particular point in time. First, it is generally acknowledged that the last two or three decades have seen a 'paradigm shift' (Gipps, 1995, p. 1) in the field of assessment. In the United Kingdom, the United States and a good many other countries around the world, the old culture of testing for purposes of comparison, selection and prediction has given way to a new culture in which the emphasis is on determining what learners actually know or can do. Even the very language of assessment has changed: today the talk is all of 'outcomes', 'competences', 'criteria' and 'attainment'. While the previous culture of testing, centred on 'constructs' and 'universes' of potential test items, typically produced scores which stood as proxies for what learners know, today the ambition is to discover what learners *actually* know.

Whilst few could object to this ambition per se, the arrangements associated with this aim have attracted considerable criticism. In particular, there is a recurring complaint that such arrangements focus more on performance than on thinking, more on behaviour than knowledge and understanding. It is thus that the lines have been drawn between, on the one hand, those who appreciate the implicit instrumentality of the new regime and, on the other, those who see such arrangements as representing a threat to the integrity of the entire educational enterprise.

The second reason why assessment has come to be a particular bone of contention of late is that around the world for the last two or three decades there has been increasing tendency for assessment to be used for the 'high-stakes' purpose of making schools and teachers accountable to governments, taxpayers and parents. While the inclination to appraise teachers 'by results' is certainly not new, the shift towards forms of assessment centred on what learners actually know or can do – as against tests designed merely to compare learners – has given weight to the idea of using assessment to hold schools and teachers to account. In the United Kingdom, the requirement to assess school pupils to determine 'what they have achieved in relation to the attainment targets' (Education Reform Act, §2, (2)c, p. 2) of the National Curriculum has been enshrined in law since 1988. And this has generally been taken to imply that 'assessment should be criterion-referenced, since its function is to ascertain achievement in relation to the ATs' (Brown, 1991, p. 215). Raising standards is central to the rationale, as is parental choice: school results are published in 'performance tables' to enable parents to make informed school choices. And there is the threat of penalties for schools officially designated as 'below the floor' (see Davis in Part 1, p. 8) by virtue of failing to achieve appropriate levels of pupil attainment or progress.

Similarly, in the United States, the early 1980s saw the move 'towards a heavily test-focused education policy' (Dwyer, 2004, p. 211). Amendments to the Elementary and Secondary Education Act (ESEA), which accompanied the introduction of the 2001 No Child Left Behind Act, mandated widespread testing arrangements and imposed penalties for schools failing to meet target levels of proficiency or unable to demonstrate sufficient progress for groups of students identified in terms of socio-economic status, race/ethnicity, disability and so on. Indeed, in both the United Kingdom and the United States, the use of high-stakes assessment has been associated both with the drive for accountability *and* a social justice agenda, assessment being seen by governments as a way of ensuring that schools serve the interests of disadvantaged or underprivileged pupils.

Yet, the use of high-stakes assessment has provoked considerable critical opposition and a catalogue of complaints. In the United Kingdom, the use of SATs (Standard Assessment Tests) has been blamed variously for narrowing the curriculum, encouraging teaching to the test and spoiling the enjoyment of education. Commentators speak of the 'tyranny' of a testing regime that has made children in England 'the most tested in the world' (Mansell, 2007, p. xiv). SATs have been accused of placing undue stress on teachers and pupils alike with one 'leading headmistress' reportedly claiming that tests were 'contributing to mental health problems among children' (Paton, 2008). Giving evidence to the House of Commons Children, Schools and Families Committee in 2008, the National Association of Schoolmasters Union of Women Teachers (NASUWT) argued that there was 'little evidence that performance tables have contributed to raising standards of attainment'. A national boycott of SATs in 2010 by both the National Union of Teachers (NUT) and the National Association of Head Teachers (NAHT) attested to deep-seated professional dissatisfaction with the testing arrangements, and there continues to be widespread concern that schools in England remain 'in thrall to data', beleaguered by a 'climate of targets, tables, and tests' (Tutt, 2012, p. 15). And such concerns are by no means confined to the teaching profession: the Director General of the Confederation of British Industry, the employers association, conveyed concerns of business leaders about the way in which some UK schools have been turned into 'exam factories' (BBC, 2012).

Much the same complaints are to be found on the other side of the Atlantic. In a Washington Post blog (Strauss, 2014), an award-winning 'veteran' teacher attacked the US government's 'obsession' with standardized tests. High-stakes testing, he claimed, is being used to 'punish teachers', is 'stifling creativity and imagination in the classroom', 'promoting a culture of cheating in many schools' and 'driving good teachers to leave their profession'.

Whether or to what extent these problems are merely contingent difficulties, potentially open to piecemeal remedy or whether they are the necessary and unavoidable consequences of high-stakes testing is a moot point. Of course, the question of whether high-stakes testing poses a *conceptual* difficulty is one which lends itself to philosophical analysis. Indeed, the entire topic of assessment should be fertile ground for philosophers, centred as it is on claims to know about the knowledgeable states of other human beings. Yet, it might be said that until relatively recently the topic of assessment has never received the philosophical attention it deserved, having, as the philosopher of education R. F. Dearden once observed, 'largely been left for the exclusive comment of psychologists' (1984, p. 123).

Andrew Davis, who provides the first contribution to this book, can be credited with having done much to remedy this neglect. In the mid-1990s, a flurry of articles appeared in the academic literature prompted by Davis's (1995) suggestion there was indeed a fundamental conceptual difficulty with the use of assessment to gauge the effectiveness of schools and teachers. Davis argued that 'no criterion-referenced assessment system can achieve both reliability and validity at the same time' (p. 3). Accordingly, assessment procedures that are sufficiently reliable will tend to 'distort proper teaching objectives concerning the development of pupil knowledge and understanding' (Davis, 1995, p. 3). The upshot is that successive governments, in striving to make educators more accountable, have imposed procedures that are not only a waste of effort and public funds, but such as are likely to have detrimental consequences for children's education. Davis thus concluded that the 'mythical goal of comparability' (p. 20) along with arrangements for the high-stakes assessment of schools and teachers should be abandoned.

Davis's 1995 paper provoked a critical response from Christopher Winch – the second contributor to this volume – and John Gingell who saw in it a kind of scepticism about the possibility of meaningful educational assessment. As they put it, Davis's position had the appearance of 'a covert project of educational nihilism' (Winch and Gingell, 1996, p. 387), an unreasonable if not cynical attempt to exempt teachers from accountability to the tax payer. They emphasized the important sense in which assessment should properly be regarded as an integral and indispensable part of the process of teaching and learning. As they put it: 'If we cannot find out whether we have done something, or how well we have done it, or how far we have got in doing it, then there seems precious little point in trying to do it' (p. 378). Now, in point of fact, there was nothing in Davis's paper which *explicitly* ruled out using assessment as a part of the process of teaching and learning. Yet, some did see in the *way* Davis framed his argument some scepticism towards the possibility of meaningful assessment. And notwithstanding this, there certainly seemed to be a need for further explanation as to how assessment which could be useful and meaningful in the context of teaching and learning necessarily became either useless or educationally damaging simply by virtue of being brought into the public realm.

Other commentators were to join the fray on either side of this debate. Davis went on to publish a book and further articles on the topic and almost a decade after Davis's original 1995 paper, the question of high-stakes assessment attracted the attention of philosophers of education on the other side of the Atlantic in a special issue of the journal *Theory and Research in Education*. If anything, the intervening years have seen both public and professional anxieties about the role of assessment in schools increase rather than lessen. And yet to this day, the matter could not be said to have arrived at any philosophical denouement. Almost two decades on, the debate amongst philosophers of education could at best be described as having reached a stalemate, a standoff between those who, like Davis, insist that there is something fundamentally ill-conceived about using assessment to hold schools and teachers to account, and those who, like Winch, remain committed to the view that assessment is an important and necessary part of any educational endeavour.

Both writers have refined and extended their arguments quite considerably for this volume. Davis offers a modified account of his position and broadens his treatment of the issue to include considerations relating to school inspection. In his response to Davis, Winch situates the question of the use of assessment for accountability purposes within a wider discussion about the purposes of educational assessment more generally, taking steps to demonstrate the variety of important and worthwhile uses to which assessment might be put, including the role of assessment within professional contexts.

In the Afterword, I broach the question of whether it might be possible to reconcile these two positions, whether it might be possible to concur with Winch as regards the vital and indispensable role of assessment in education whilst at the same time acknowledging Davis's intuition that there is something fundamentally wrong-headed about using assessment to hold schools and teachers to account. I will suggest that in order to reconcile these seemingly incompatible positions and resolve this apparent impasse, it is necessary to challenge some long held assumptions about the very nature of assessment. In the meantime, I leave it to Davis and Winch to present their respective cases, which in the context of current thinking about educational assessment could be said to represent the two grand and antithetical readings of our time.

Part One

Assessment and Accountability

Andrew Davis

Introduction

Educational assessment has, and should have, many constructive purposes. Yet, one particular purpose has dominated in much of the developed world in the last few decades – to hold teachers and schools to account. Tests are used to 'measure' the quality of the education system. This has a destructive effect on education, even if the main aim for education is considered to be the preparation of employees in a competitive industrial economy. I show in detail why assessment should not be used to hold education to account, arguing that the importance of 'real' or 'rich' knowledge in the curriculum is constantly threatened by accountability pressures. I end by exploring other ways of holding education and teachers to account.

Standards, accountability and 'real knowledge'

High-stakes assessment dominates education in much of the developed world, especially in the United States and in England.

Tests are venerated as icons of the quality and effectiveness of schools and other educational institutions. Results are used to hold educators to account. Assessment has been made to *matter* in all kinds of ways for schools, their teachers and indeed to the public at large. League tables comparing English schools' test performances have been a potent symbol of this approach since the 1990s.

Many educators have long believed that assessment should have different purposes. They hold, for instance, that we should focus on 'assessment for learning' rather than assessment for accountability. Teachers who carry out 'assessment for learning' want to discover their students' understanding levels and motivation. They do this in order to make properly informed decisions about their teaching. They seek to take account of students' existing knowledge, difficulties and interest levels so that they can pitch their explanations and tasks accordingly. Their continuous monitoring may include tests, but much of it comprises informal observation of student responses during classroom interactions. Where appropriate, teachers supply their students with feedback, designed to support and promote further learning. Some psychologists speak of 'dynamic assessment' in this connection. The authors of the well-known 'Inside the Black Box' contribution to the assessment debate are sympathetic:

> We start from the self-evident proposition that teaching and learning have to be interactive. Teachers need to know about their pupils' progress and difficulties with learning so that they can adapt their work to meet their needs – needs which are often unpredictable and which vary from one pupil to another. (Black and Wiliam, 2001, p. 1)

Nevertheless, the UK Coalition government shows little sign of lowering the assessment stakes. Consider, for instance, the Department for Education's introduction of the unlovely expression 'below the floor':

> 6.26 For secondary schools, a school will be below the floor if fewer than 35 per cent of pupils achieve the 'basics' standard of 5 A*-C grade GCSEs including English and mathematics, and fewer pupils make good progress between key stage two and key

stage four than the national average. For primary schools, a school will be below the floor if fewer than 60 per cent of pupils achieve the 'basics' standard of level four in both English and mathematics and fewer pupils than average make the expected levels of progress between key stage one and key stage two. (Department for Education, 2011)

A school 'below the floor' is judged to be offering poor quality education. Note the continuing element of 'progress measurement' and the equation, in effect, of school quality with examination results. Incidentally, 'floor standards' for primary schools change in 2014, requiring 65 per cent in the 'basic standards'. From 2016, secondary school 'floor standards' will involve 'measured progress' in eight subjects.

For many decades, critics of high-stakes assessment have been unable to convince government that its use of testing is gravely flawed. In particular, critics have urged that it is not possible to employ a given assessment task both for accountability purposes and to generate information that helps teachers to support the learning of the particular group of students who have attempted the task (see, e.g., Stobart, 2001).

Those opposing high-stakes assessment would not object to tests that *sample* the achievements of a national cohort of students, where the resulting data is returned to schools and is not offered to external agencies. Such a process can, of course, be very helpful to teachers. They may well be able to take account of the results when revising and refining their *general* pedagogical approaches to the curriculum content concerned. However, this would not be high stakes in the classic sense: no particular schools or teachers would be directly affected as a result of their pupils' performances.

In the United Kingdom, the Task Group on Assessment and Testing (TGAT), whose work informed the shape of the National Curriculum assessment framework, failed to come clean about the tensions between different assessment functions. For instance, they observed:

It is possible to build up a comprehensive picture of the overall achievements of a pupil by aggregating, in a structured way, the separate results of a set of assessments designed to serve formative purposes. However, if assessments were designed only for summative purposes, then formative information could not be obtained, since the summative assessments occur at the end of a phase of learning and make no attempt at throwing light on the educational history of the pupil. It is realistic to envisage, for the purpose of evaluation, ways of aggregating the information on individual pupils into accounts of the success of a school, or LEA, in facilitating the learning and achievements of those for whom it is responsible; again, the reverse process is an impossibility. (DES 1987, para 25)

This gave the impression that combining accountability and formative purposes was perfectly feasible, and that the only issue worthy of comment was that of timing.

The history of assessment in England since the TGAT report raises many questions, including the following. Suppose it had been apparent from the outset that National Curriculum assessments' formative purpose could not in fact be realized. Would resistance to their high-stakes function have been stronger and more effective? National Curriculum test data were supposed to help teachers support their students' learning. Arguably, this has never actually happened. The early versions of the standard tasks were potentially valuable in that they were often practical and resembled other classroom activities: detailed information from the pupils' responses could certainly be used formatively. However, as part of a statutory framework applicable to all pupils, they involved huge workload demands for teachers and were abandoned in favour of pencil and paper tests (see, e.g., Black, 1994 for some of this history).

Criticisms of assessment for accountability have been advanced in many developed countries. They have been elaborated by practising teachers and by researchers from a wide variety of disciplines. Singling out any one of these critics is arbitrary, but I cannot resist Donald Campbell in 1976:

The more any quantitative social indicator is used for social decision-making, the more subject it will be to corruption pressures and the more apt it will be to distort and corrupt the social processes it is intended to monitor... when test scores become the goal of the teaching process, they both lose their value as indicators of educational status and distort the educational process in undesirable ways. (Campbell, 1976, p. 35)

Opposition to National Curriculum testing has not been universal. Some supporters see a positive relationship between testing and the quality of schooling. However, I suspect that such views are in the minority among educators, though I am much less confident about public opinion more generally.

Politicians require visible successes in the short term, so it is easy to understand that they find it expedient to emphasize improving test scores. The latter can be paraded in front of the public as 'indicators' of 'successful' educational policies. But, why have so many of the *rest* of us been taken in by such an insidious equation of test results and 'standards'?

Perhaps these issues have not been sufficiently explored at the level of first principles. In my contribution to this book, I intend to remedy this omission. I hope to generate the kind of understanding that might finally bring people to their senses.

In what follows, I mainly deal with the problems. A full discussion of the constructive uses of assessment (and, of course, there are many) will not be attempted here. Note that it is difficult to avoid offering some opinions about the actual consequences of high-stakes assessment. It is beyond the scope of my contribution to this book to offer appropriate evidence for these opinions. So, readers seeking verdicts that can be justified by appealing to empirical evidence should look elsewhere.

What ought governments to believe to justify their continuing defence of high-stakes testing? They should certainly claim the existence of a strong relationship between, on the one hand, the realization of their preferred educational aims, and on the other hand, educational assessment with all it implies for school students' teaching and learning experiences. So, what aims for education is the modern state likely to favour? In all probability, it will feel that pupils should be prepared for their fate as employees in a competitive industrial economy. In developing a critique of contemporary assessment policy, I assume, for the sake of argument, that this answer is defensible. I want to explore the problems that arise *even if* such a contestable vision for education is taken for granted.

On such an approach, the State should understand 'improvement' to mean rather more than the fact, if it is a fact, that test scores have increased for given age groups over the last few years. It ought to believe that rising performances indicate that students, in their ultimate adult roles, will *really* know more, understand more and be able to do more than earlier generations of students in the corresponding age groups. Improvements in test results per se should have no value, either for policy makers or, indeed, for the general public.

Now, if beliefs in a close and explicitly specifiable relationship between better test scores and real improvements in adult knowledge can be shown to be unsound, then the focus on league tables and other high-stakes phenomena is exposed as irrational and perverse. I intend to argue in some detail that the beliefs in question are indeed unsound where assessment is used for accountability purposes.

To pursue such a demonstration, I turn first to an exploration of what is meant here by 'real knowledge' and 'genuine knowledge improvement'. Suppose, for instance, I 'know' that Michael Faraday discovered the dynamo. What would 'real knowledge' amount to in this example? Without awareness of many other things, including dynamos, electricity, science in general and the relationships between these and my Michael Faraday material, I can do nothing with the latter except to regurgitate it on demand. Evidently, the linkage between a specific piece of knowledge and other knowledge will not be an all-or-nothing affair. It will be a matter of degree. As pupils learn and mature, we would expect the 'connectedness' of their knowledge to develop in accuracy, comprehensiveness and sophistication. I would want to characterize knowledge backed by 'connections' as 'real' knowledge, and knowledge that I can only use to answer an appropriately phrased question as 'thin'.

I require knowledge, understanding and skills of various kinds to deal with everyday events and work place challenges. Without appropriate connections between a given piece of knowledge and much else that I know, it will be 'in' my mind without being understood. It cannot be applied to a range of contexts in daily life and in the workplace. Perhaps all I can do is to answer a test question correctly. 'Real' knowledge is knowledge that is connected, at least to some degree. It is knowledge possessed with at least some measure of understanding, and hence, it can inform my activities in the world. For substantial understanding, I require a 'cognitive map', in which the specific knowledge in question is appropriately situated, where routes to related concepts are accurate and where I have a good appreciation of their character.

Consider the kind of adult literacy really worth having. It must be applicable in a virtually limitless diversity of contexts. I (reluctantly) read tax forms, overdue gas bills, books and on-screen information from a database or the Internet. I complete application forms for jobs and compose letters to my friends and relatives. I extract (with difficulty) the meaning from flat pack instruction leaflets and I enter material sensibly in a computer database.

What of numeracy? I calculate mentally, sometimes rounding up or down to produce an approximate answer when that is sufficient. On encountering a 'real life' problem requiring some arithmetic, such as which mortgage package best suits my needs, I recognize whether to add, subtract, multiply, divide or use some combination. With bigger numbers, decimals and complex situations, I may use a calculator or computer. Before I calculate, I have a rough idea of the answer. This helps me to identify possible slips, whether in my mental arithmetic or in my use of technology. To perform intelligent estimates and select appropriate operations, I need to appreciate the links between addition and subtraction, multiplication and division, and how the whole number system works.

Both literacy and numeracy also depend for their successful application on a range of practical skills. It would be perfectly possible to teach pupils to be theoretically literate and numerate, but who, because of their practical inadequacies, could not actually apply their knowledge to their encounters with the world.

In short, I cannot be intelligently literate and numerate unless I have formed links in my mind between relevant items of knowledge and concepts. Arguably, government should have reason to believe that both test performance and preparation are *closely and predictably* associated with the development of such connected knowledge. After all, it is well aware that in a high-stakes assessment regime, curriculum coverage and approaches will be strongly influenced by the content and style of the relevant tests. That is to say, there will be extensive 'teaching to the test'.

So, enhanced test preparation and performance had better contribute to improving connected knowledge. The connectedness of my knowledge is, arguably, bound up very closely with whether I can transfer it from the situations in which I originally acquired it to contexts I encounter in my everyday life and in the workplace. Transfer is traditionally defined as the influence of prior learning on performance in a new situation. Construed in this fashion, it permeates our very existence: without it, learning could never take place. If someone learns to ride a bike in her backyard, she may well succeed in riding it down the road tomorrow. If, today, a child can answer correctly an addition question such as 2 + 3, she should succeed with 5 + 2 tomorrow, and perhaps even realize that she needs £5 when buying a couple of presents, one of which costs £2 and another £3.

I cannot transfer my knowledge from one context to another without a degree of connectedness. Suppose for a moment that my knowledge that Faraday discovered the dynamo is little more than an example of rote learning. It is 'in' my mind in some sense, but I make few if any connections between the idea of a dynamo and my understanding of electricity, between Faraday and notions of science, scientists, the Victorian era and so on. So, if a pupil asks me about how electricity is generated, and how the whole ingenious process began, I fail to bring my Faraday knowledge into the conversation. I do not transfer that knowledge to the conversation with my pupil, because I do not appreciate the relevant links.

The relationship between transfer and the connectedness of my knowledge works both ways. Without a measure of transfer, my knowledge cannot possess any degree of connectedness. If I cannot bring my Faraday knowledge into the conversation with my pupil, this transfer failure means that I do not connect the Faraday knowledge with the ideas and concepts being explored with my pupil.

Preparing for examinations and examination achievements ought to contribute to knowledge that *transfers* predictably and comprehensively to daily life and the workplace. If it does not, we are hardly dealing with improving standards.

Now, to what extent, if at all, are the activities associated with the drive to improve test scores also promoting 'real' or 'connected' knowledge? As I have just said, the question about transfer is inextricably bound up with the question about knowledge 'connectedness'. So, I can, in effect, address both connectedness and transfer by pursuing the latter, and this is what I now intend to do. What is the relationship between the focus on high-stakes assessment and transfer?

There is considerable evidence that pupils triumphing in given contexts do *not* always achieve in others that seem 'similar', or to involve the 'same' knowledge, skill or competence. What counts as being the same, or being similar in such situations? This is a much more complicated question than it seems. Some theorists emphasize the role of context and situation in defining the very identity of someone's knowledge or ability. Here is just one example from researchers in the 'situated cognition' tradition:

> Children's representations of mathematics draw from the particular social and physical activities in which they engage (buying and selling, comparing, measuring, etc.). Their ways of conceiving and doing mathematics owe much to the specific representations and tools they learn to use such as abacus, weights and measures, notational systems, and so forth. (Carraher and Schliemann, 2002, p. 4)

Just how are we to understand such claims? One way of construing such observations results in a radical reading: items of knowledge and activities in one situation, tied as they are to the particulars of the social practices in which that situation is embedded, frequently *differ fundamentally* from those in a second situation. On such a radical reading this is so, even where abstract similarities seem to obtain between the two situations and where what is known in each situation can apparently be expressed in the same words. For instance, in the famous study of Brazilian street children (Nunes et al., 1993) teenagers used a range of calculations when engaged in street trading, looking after cars and so on. In school, they encountered arithmetic that could be appropriately described, at least in abstract terms, in the same way as that which they were using in the streets, namely multi-digit addition, subtraction, multiplication and division. Yet, on the radical reading under consideration, the 'school mathematics' differed fundamentally from the 'street mathematics'.

What are we to make of the status of such readings? They surely transcend those that could be settled simply by appealing to relevant empirical evidence. Deciding what counts as the same knowledge and what does not takes us into philosophical territory. As noted above, we encounter mixed fortunes when we attempt to make detailed predictions about transfer. This fact, together with our difficulties in the face of differing verdicts on similarities and differences between contexts, knowledge and performances, points to deep conceptual problems here, or so I believe. Evidence of surprising transfer failures *and* successes is a symptom[1] of this situation.

This issue is fundamental when considering the relationship between test performances on the one hand, and adult knowledge and capability on the other. I now want to argue that it is impossible *in principle* to specify this relationship in any kind of detail, and that this limitation springs from the conceptual problems I have just mentioned. My conclusion has important implications for the health of high-stakes assessment.

Consider some examples. We make judgements about whether English required in the workplace closely resembles school English, or about the extent to which an everyday life context requiring the application of some physics is similar to, or differs from, the contexts of school physics. On the basis of such verdicts, we then predict the likelihood of transfer.

Psychologists distinguish between 'near transfer' and 'far transfer'. So, for instance, a school very concerned about the vocational 'relevance' of its curriculum and examinations might, after careful

---

[1]For evidence relating to the 'transfer' of mathematics learning, see, for instance, Ruthven (1987) and the Assessment of Performance Unit's work on this subject, summarized in Assessment of Performance Unit (1985). A psychologist offering extensive evidence on this topic is S. J. Ceci. See, for instance, Ceci and Roazzi, (1994) or Ceci (1996).

consideration, choose to use a specific exam board. This might be on the grounds that the test tasks were a 'good match' for those their pupils would meet in the workplace. Hence, the school could be characterized as believing that, on the basis of its selected board, only 'near' transfer from typical examination tasks would be required for success in the workplace. 'Near transfer' is to be contrasted with 'far transfer'. In the case of the latter, learning in a given context influences success in future situations that appear to be very different from the initial learning context. For instance, suppose someone thought that developing skills on the school rugger field would increase the probability of future success as an accountant. This would be an implausible belief about 'far transfer', since accountancy and rugger seem to have very little in common.

Let us continue to reflect on these ideas of 'near' and 'far' as applied to transfer, together with judgements of sameness and similarity when applied to contexts and tasks. On cursory reflection, we may well assume that our conceptions of sameness and similarity here can happily be modelled on those we apply to natural objects and processes. What are those conceptions? For instance, a scientist might note the properties of water in a bottle at room temperature in Durham on a January day. It is liquid, colourless, clear and so on. The bottle is then transported to a new context. It is 'transferred'. The new context is a St. Petersburg park. The scientist observes, among other things, that it is no longer liquid, that it takes up more room than it did when liquid and that it is no longer transparent. She notes that the temperature was 17°C in the Durham laboratory, whereas it is −10°C in the Russian park. She can make precise objective measurements of the similarities and differences between the original context and the new Russian context, and of the properties of the bottle's contents in each of the situations. These similarities and differences are independent of the scientist's particular culture and values. They have nothing to do with the social practices in which she is embedded, and they obtain independently of human decision-making.

Yet, in contrast, whether one human action, performance or context is similar to another usually implicates aspects of the social and cultural practices in which the actors are situated. I want to illustrate this point through several examples.

In the first, we are dealing with social practices, rules or conventions that create the very possibility of actions of certain kinds in given contexts. Games illustrate this point beautifully. You can move a small castle-shaped object on a board featuring alternating black and white squares, having eight squares on each side of the board. You can slide the object along the rows and columns of black and white squares. However, if these moves are to count as *moving a rook*, you need the rules of chess in force. (Searle, 1995 calls these rules *constitutive* and credits Rawls, 1955 with the idea.) Chess pieces differ from one set to another, and boards vary in size. Some players will lift the rook from its square and 'plant' it on its destination, while others might slide it or push it along for half the journey and lift it for the other half. Such a set of potentially disparate physical actions becomes 'similar' to each other by virtue of exemplifying chess moves.

I now move on to my second example. Mary, a police officer on traffic duty, raises her hand, palm forward. She is directing oncoming traffic to stop. Later in the day, in a different part of the town, John, another policeman, gestures with his hand to give a similar message. Both officers' actions are instances of 'directing oncoming traffic to stop'. Thus categorized, it is implied that the performances are similar in certain respects. The implied similarities would not exist, however, without the existence in the relevant community of a *convention* that certain hand movements in such contexts *count* as indicating to oncoming traffic that it should stop. Considered *physically*, Mary's gestures may well differ from John's in some ways. Now compare John and Mary's performances with that of Brown's – a reporter in a war zone who emerges from a building into a crowd of hostile men. He holds up his hand as a sign of peace. So, Brown's hand movement, though in some ways physically similar to Mary's and to John's, does *not* constitute a signal to traffic. There is at least one significant category to which Mary's and John's actions belong, and Brown's does not. In an important sense, then, Brown's action is *not* similar to Mary's and John's.

In the third example, whether one action is similar to another cannot be separated from the values of the culture in which it is performed. What counts as intelligent performance varies from one community to another, and calling actions or people intelligent is partly a matter of making a value judgement. Members of the

Kpelle tribe in Africa were given a sorting task. When what we deem 'intelligent' people in our culture are given the task of sorting creatures, for instance, they will typically put all the fish together, classify both these and birds as animals and so on. In short, they build up a hierarchy. The Kpelle tribe refused to sort like this until they were asked to complete the task as a foolish person would. They immediately sorted hierarchically (Sternberg, 1999). In this case, then, how an action is categorized depends to some extent on the prevailing cultural *norms*. Intelligence is not a feature which actions possess *independently* of cultural and social contexts.

The fourth and final example is an even more complex case taken from teaching itself, involving what counts as 'explaining' (Davis, 1999). Suppose teaching is held to involve 'explaining' only when the pupils actually acquire relevant knowledge – a stipulation which, you might think, should not provoke too much controversy. Yet there are complications. The teaching profession and the wider community are not in complete agreement about what is to count as knowing. Some want to build in the ability to manifest the said knowledge in a wide and unbounded variety of ways, implying that 'connected' understanding is an indispensable component of knowing. For instance, a science teacher might develop her students' knowledge of force by setting up experiments with spring balances, to provoke conflict between students' existing ideas about force and those that they encounter by experimenting. She believes that this 'constructivist' approach is one way of encouraging the development of 'connected' knowledge. She construes knowledge as incorporating a measure of connectedness, and this is why she plans the style of physics lesson just sketched.

Others have a very different approach, feeling that knowledge can be specified in terms of appropriate answers to relevant questions. The conception of knowledge in certain game.shows, for instance, involves the participants' capacity to produce specified responses.

Evidently, the majority of knowledge conceptions in contemporary society lie somewhere between these two extremes. People need not have fixed views about these matters and may not even be consistent from one context or subject to another.

So, verdicts on whether a teacher's actions count as 'explaining' will relate in complex ways to beliefs in the relevant communities about what constitutes knowledge, and indeed much else. Whether one teaching performance, then, is *similar* to another is not a question that can be answered without reference to the social environments of the performances. Such environments vary in many ways – some aspects may be relatively stable over time and be found across many societies and cultures, while others have a short life. Even within a particular social group or school staff, some social conventions and practices may conflict with others or interact in complex ways.

In addition, questions about what counts as *knowing* something cannot be separated from how this knowledge would be shown. We discover what people know by observing what they say and do in a range of contexts. We have just seen that how an action should be characterized (explaining rather than telling, acting intelligently rather than stupidly, conferring a degree on a student rather than insulting a Moslem woman by grasping her hand, and so on) is bound up with complex and shifting features of the social and cultural environment. This point applies as much to actions that manifest knowledge as to any other actions. There are crucial implications here for the fundamental character of knowledge. It appears that knowledge is not merely an individual asset, but rather a state of affairs involving individuals *in their social and cultural environment*.

I can now return to the main argument of this section. How closely do test performances and the associated knowledge 'resemble' that involved in everyday life and the work place? The answer depends, at least to some degree, upon fluctuating and possibly fragmented social and cultural features in which the relevant performances are embedded. The adult contexts themselves may not have anything common to *all* of them. The differences between them are complex, subtle and sometimes elusive. Not all of them are stable over time. They will include unwritten rules about how to go about answering questions in tests and hosts of other social features. In the work place, pragmatic, economic and legal issues will interact in intricate fashion, both with each other and with the relevant actions of employees.

The relevant sociocultural environment incorporates large numbers of shifting judgements about what counts as 'the same' knowledge, skill, content and about related values. Even within a particular community or educational institution, there may well be no consensus in such judgements. People are often only tacitly aware of the kinds of complexities to which I have just referred. They may be unable to articulate and codify them.

So, whether a particular performance is 'of the same kind' as an earlier one, or whether the 'same knowledge' as last time is required this time, cannot be established in a simple and straightforward manner. There just is no comparison here with the task of examining the similarities and differences between a bottle of water and its physical environment on a January day in Durham, and that bottle when transferred to St. Petersburg. The resemblances between school knowledge, performances and contexts on the one hand, and adult life knowledge, performances and contexts on the other, do not subsist independently of human activity and meanings. They are tied to complex, sometimes impermanent and ambiguous human decisions and practices. The intractable character of these difficulties cannot be removed by scrutinizing the knowledge or performance itself more closely. For the identities of the relevant actions are bound up with the sociocultural contexts in which they occur. Again, the point is not the absurd one that transfer does not occur, but rather that it resists attempts to capture it in any kind of detail and accuracy.

So, I am certainly not denying, for instance, that there is likely to be *some* association between competence in school English tests and what we would call English proficiency in a range of real-life contexts in which adults find themselves. Of course there is. To repeat, transfer happens. I *am* attacking the idea that such links are invariably self-evident, fine-grained and precisely detectable.

Confidence in the existence of links of the kind I am disputing would have to rest on beliefs in a robust notion of similarity akin to that available in natural science, the type of similarity that is independent of social and cultural environments. Yet, in *human* situations such kinds of similarity are rarely to be found.

Incidentally, I have never held an 'extreme non-transferability' view that would question the very possibility of transfer. Yet, despite my repeated attempts to clarify this point, some commentators still interpret me in this way – for instance, Winch, 2010. However, in Davis 1998, I said that 'It would be foolish to deny that there *will* be transfer between school success and employee competence'. Davis, 1999, observes, 'This is not to say that transfer never occurs. Of course it does. Indeed, without transfer some would argue that learning could scarcely go on' (p. 8). Davis, 2010, noted, 'if we attempted to deny transfer we would be committed to a manifestly absurd position' (p. 324).

Be that as it may, another approach to this issue focuses on terms such as 'ability', 'skill' or 'competence'. We can readily coin phrases that appear to refer to psychological items of these kinds. Examples include 'critical thinking skills', 'problem solving abilities' and 'caring skills'. We may assume that these phrases can refer to assets which people can acquire and retain. If so, our thinking likens such putative traits to something like 'ball throwing ability'. The latter *does* seem to pick out a feature that someone could develop and maintain over a period of time. We see Jones throwing balls in various situations and conclude that he has the ability to throw a ball. This implies that he will succeed in throwing balls in future if the circumstances are right and he wants to. That is, the ball-throwing is expected to transfer to future occasions where Jones, in an appropriate frame of mind, performs in contexts resembling those in which we have already observed him. Here, we would be dealing with cases of 'near' transfer. Of course, confidence would decline if he were being asked to throw under water or to throw a metal ball weighing 5 kg. Were he to succeed in the latter cases, we might regard these as instances of 'far' transfer.

Our trust in our transfer predictions is reasonably grounded on the fact that Jones's performances are actually open to observation, the judgement that his skills are explicable in terms of adequately functioning musculature, senses and brain, and the assumption that these physical features can persist over periods of time. We can readily identify his actions as being of a given kind, where the categories we employ concern the physical properties of the performances. We can say a good deal about his actions by using descriptions which apply to them regardless of the sociocultural environment in which he is situated.

Now, many educational uses of 'ability', 'skill' or 'competence' aspire to identify achievements that are far more complex and open to interpretation than the straightforward 'ball-throwing ability'. We need to understand in some detail the difficulties here. A classic example is provided by 'problem solving ability'. Perhaps Jane, a Year-11 pupil, cleans a sparking plug in the car in the school engineering workshop, replaces a fuse in an electric soldering iron, charges a flat battery in the school video camera and helps a teacher to remember where he left his reading glasses. Each of these might be described as practical problem-solving. So, we might say that Jane has a practical problem-solving ability (Davis, 1988).

What does our judgement signify? On one interpretation, we may be speaking of Jane's customary enthusiasm for practical tasks, the fact that she wastes no time in embarking on them, and that she rarely if ever leaves a job half done. In short, we may be attributing to her a positive attitude to practical tasks. That, of course, is quite important and might go some way to justify our confidence in her when she encounters a new problem. Nevertheless, we are talking in very general terms here. On a second interpretation, we are merely summarizing previous achievements, and so talk of a problem-solving ability is just an example of harmless shorthand. These two interpretations are not mutually exclusive.

Any attempts to make *detailed* predictions of future successes in virtue of Jane's possession of some kind of 'problem-solving muscle' should be treated with scepticism. This is because the various examples where Jane has solved problems need have nothing in common. Suppose we set aside Jane's general attitude to solving problems as a possible explanation of her successes. What other reasons could be brought into play? After all, relevant knowledge and understanding might be specific to each achievement. No limits could be set on the physical actions that might figure. Indeed, some problems can be 'solved' without performing any physical actions at all. Moreover, as we saw earlier in our exploration of transfer, the very categories into which Jane's actions are placed often reflect contingent and fluctuating cultural norms. The invention of the phrase 'problem-solving ability' in effect seeks to conjure into existence a psychological trait guaranteeing transfer. Empirical research indicates that this 'folk psychology' style of thinking about personal traits is deeply entrenched.

Analysis of a simple mathematical case highlights the insubstantial character of these abilities, skills or competences. At first sight, mathematics may appear to be relatively cut and dried, and the business of attributing basic numeracy skills to pupils perfectly straightforward, at least in comparison with cases such as problem-solving or advanced writing. However, now consider the alleged ability to subtract. A pupil can answer correctly whenever she is presented with 12–5 as a written symbolic calculation in horizontal format. Yet, a 'subtraction competence' would need to amount to rather more than this. Perhaps she also ought to succeed when the subtraction appears in vertical form. Now, suppose we ask her the question in conversation rather than writing it for her. Imagine further that terms other than 'take away' are used. How will she respond to 'subtract', 'minus' or 'difference'? So far, we have restricted ourselves to one specific subtraction calculation. But of course, she needs to be able to deal with the subtraction of any numbers. Do we have an upper limit in mind? Should we include fractions and decimals? What about offering an example such as 5–12? Imagine that we turn aside from subtraction problems in the abstract and, instead, suggest challenges in realistic contexts that require subtraction of some kind to be solved.

Suppose we are supremely confident that she will be able to meet *all* these demands. What could possibly legitimate such confidence? It could not be justified without certain convictions about transfer; these beliefs in turn perhaps buttressed by the thought that our pupil has some kind of underlying 'subtraction muscle'. (Obviously we do not use the term 'subtraction muscle'. It is simply a vivid phrase that captures the type of thinking at work here. The idea seems to be that the pupil has an individual asset or feature which she can carry with her from one context to another – just as she has a particular blood group and genetic constitution, whatever the context in which she finds herself.)

Nevertheless, much of this whole story depends on those notions of 'same' and 'similar' that we have already seen fit to question – on the idea that resemblances and differences somehow exist wholly independently of our interests, judgements and social conventions. We assert, for instance, that what must go on to solve 5–12 (or –3–8, or even –2 – –10) is 'similar' in some sense to that required for 10–6. Such assertions may be questioned. For a strong case could be made for the claim that, in some ways, the conception of subtraction involved in 5–12 must 'differ' from conceptions that would be sufficient in all those cases where the answer is greater than zero. Whatever conclusions we come to about these difficult issues, mere assertion will not spirit subtraction abilities into existence, nor bring about transfer just because the knowledge or operation required seems so similar.

A recent twist of UK government policy raises even more questions about the transfer issue. The former Education Secretary, Michael Gove, is outlawing modular GCSEs and the practice of allowing course work to count towards the examination grade. Instead, students will have to take a final exam at the end of the two-year course. One reason given for abandoning modular structures is that they led to a high number of retakes.

Now, just why is there supposed to be a problem about retaking an examination? There certainly may be issues of cost here. Of much greater importance is the argument that if students are focused on tests for much of the time, then their learning is distorted. Gove offered the latter as one of the reasons for the decision to turn away from modular exams.

> Those bits could be resat. That meant instead of concentrating on teaching and learning you had people who were being trained again and again to clear the hurdle of the examination along the way. That meant that unfortunately less time was being spent developing a deep and rounded knowledge of the subject. (Gove, reported in BBC news 2011a)

There is a wonderful irony here. Concerns about devaluing 'deep and rounded knowledge' have been at the heart of the objections most frequently mounted against high-stakes assessment in the last few decades. Yet, Gove appears to have no intention of abandoning assessment for accountability.

In any event, I suspect that the reasons he cites are not the only reasons or even the real reasons, especially given the link he is seeking to establish between 'rigour' and the policy to award a key role to final examinations (BBC, 2011). Is there a feeling that if a student achieves a pass grade after several tries, this is less worthwhile than one awarded on the first occasion? If such a feeling does exist, is it justified? After all, if test results are supposed to be satisfactory indicators of 'real knowledge', on what evidence can it be claimed that results from the first occasion on which the test is taken are better indicators of such knowledge than performance on the fifth occasion? Indeed, why not assume, for instance, that the efforts required for the retakes that ultimately result in a pass, at the same time, contribute to the development of genuine knowledge? Why not judge that immediate success might actually be a disadvantage because it could be achieved before candidates have sufficient time to develop rich knowledge?

Please do not misunderstand me here. It is not that that I favour repeated retakes. In practice, there may be all kinds of problems with modularization and lots of small tests. It is rather that I am suspicious of the motives behind current policy decisions. I sometimes wonder whether opposition to retakes may stem from a tacit scepticism about the link between examination results, transfer to real-world challenges and genuine knowledge. If someone does not believe in such links, they might possibly think that in reality examinations are or should be about something else, namely sorting the sheep from the goats. According to such thinking, the population is made up of individuals with varying degrees of 'intelligence', this construed as a fixed trait on the basis of which people are appropriately to be judged more, or less, valuable. It is assumed that 'intelligent' people will pass the examination on the very first occasion they take it. Yet, the system that permitted repeated retakes allowed the 'less intelligent' to *obtain the same results as their 'superior' fellow citizens*. In the kind of thinking about which I am speculating here, this amounts to a 'dumbing down' of 'standards'.

Sentiments such as these relate in turn to a long-standing dislike of the philosophy of criterion-referenced assessment per se. According to the latter, students should be graded according to whether they meet given criteria, these allegedly relating to their possession of specified knowledge and understanding. Such an approach allows for the possibility that, over time, more and more students will achieve the highest grades. The dislike of assessment policy based on tests seeking to measure 'absolute' levels of knowledge and understanding is linked to an attachment to a norm-referenced approach, according to which grades will reflect, not absolute achievement, but how well the student is performing in relation to the rest of the cohort taking the examination. This means that those with the highest grades remain 'special', being members of a select group. There will never be any danger that they will be 'swamped' by inferior students 'catching up'.

To sum up, it follows from the problems about transfer and the mythological character of much discourse concerning abilities, competences and skills, that the global identification of 'raising standards' with improving test performance cannot be justified. Our capacities to capture and predict the relationships between test performances and allegedly associated 'real-life' knowledge and activity are limited in principle.

If only society, and the state in particular, could bring itself to appreciate this point, then the utilitarian requirements of adult citizens destined to contribute to a flourishing industrial economy would no longer need to dominate *detailed* decisions about curriculum content and approaches to teaching and learning. Values of different kinds might, once more, have a really significant influence on these choices. Working with others, using imagination, developing critical and creative thinking and the expressive arts in general could resume an appropriately high-profile position in every school. Of course, even now, most schools need no lessons on the importance of these things and strive to place them at the heart of their educational provision. Nevertheless, they constantly have to fend off the pressures of assessment.

Paradoxically, enriching the current curriculum in this way might turn out to serve the needs of an industrial economy at least as well as a narrow focus on test preparation and test taking.

Teaching to the test issues

The discussion so far has, in effect, explored one aspect of the venerable problem of 'teaching to the test'. I now turn to a direct examination of this subject. It is important to understand that 'teaching to the test' is susceptible of a variety of interpretations. In some guises, it turns out to be a good idea, educationally speaking. We need to appreciate why it sometimes damages teaching and learning, without making the assumption that it is always to be deplored.

Many tests and examinations are repeated year after year. Examples include National Curriculum tests in England and SAT subject tests in the United States. Each fresh version of the tests is supposed to be 'equivalent' to previous versions in terms of content and difficulty levels. One simple way of achieving such equivalence would be to feature exactly the same test questions each time. Needless to say, in the real world, few if any agencies dealing with academic subjects use exactly the same questions each time. If we look at tests of 'non-academic' capabilities, however, the situation is rather different.

Associated Board Music exams require candidates to play the same scales and arpeggios for a particular grade. The tasks remain unaltered for years on end. Candidates will be tested on a sample of what is on the syllabus only, but they have an exact knowledge of the finite set of tasks from which the examiner can choose. Equally, a test of whether a swimmer can complete 10 lengths of the baths is quite specific, remains the same whether taken now or in six months time and should hold no surprises for the candidate. The driving test is close to the swimming and music cases, although drivers are put through their paces in a wide range of places and weather conditions, so perhaps it would not be entirely correct to say that it repeats exactly the 'same' tasks for all those subjecting themselves to it.

Suppose a driving instructor or instrumental music teacher engages in 'teaching to the test' – that is, they teach by ensuring that their students attempt just those tasks that will be required of them in the test, and they provide their pupils with appropriate support and feedback during these attempts. Far from complaining to the teacher about her approach, most students and parents would be only too pleased.

Compare these examples with tests of academic knowledge and understanding where the familiar contention that 'teaching to the test' is educationally unacceptable seems to be more persuasive. Were the same test to be offered on each occasion, teachers could, under the pressures of accountability, attempt to ensure that their students would succeed in the relevant tasks *regardless of what they understood.*

Rehearsing this possibility invokes and assumes a 'gap' between test performance on the one hand, and underlying knowledge and understanding on the other. Now, where the intended learning outcome is, for instance, playing the scale of A major on the piano, there seems to be no such 'gap'. Surely, success is just performing an action of a specific kind, namely playing the relevant scale. It is true that some performers might, as they play, ponder how A major relates to other keys, or reflect on important compositions written in that particular key. Others might even wonder whether there are sausages for tea. But of course, these psychological states are not assessed. They are irrelevant to the performance.

In contrast, imagine an arithmetic test in which the items were additions and subtractions of three digit numbers such as 244 + 576 and 907 − 268. It would be possible to prepare pupils by teaching them traditional algorithms − sets of rules which, if followed properly, would enable the right answers to be obtained. It may be appropriate to teach some pupils such algorithms. Yet, if that is all they know, as opposed to being in possession of a good understanding of the number system, place value and the relationships between the various arithmetic operations, they will be unable to apply their arithmetic to everyday problems, and may be incapable of using alternative routes to the correct answer, such as mentally counting up from 268 to 907, to carry out the subtraction calculation. 'Teaching to the test' could consist simply of training in the algorithms. Few teachers would judge that this would be appropriate content and pedagogy if it dominated their teaching. Nevertheless, the 'high-stakes' pressure may influence at least some practitioners in this direction.

So, all academic examiners ply their trade in the context of a classic theoretical dilemma. They could, in principle, create questions which closely resemble each other from year to year, on the grounds that this is the obvious way of testing the 'same knowledge' or the 'same abilities, skills and competences' over time. Let us refer to this as the 'similar question option'. Some will feel that there is a lot to be said for this option. For, if examiners *don't* assess the 'same thing' year on year, then there is no simple and straightforward way of talking about standards over time, at least on the basis of test results.[2] Some politicians and other policy makers fervently wish to talk about standards over time. On just this kind of basis, they are disposed to wax lyrical about their track records.

The contrasting option would be to *vary* test items. Examiners could decide that, over successive versions of the tests, they would offer a wide range of either written or practical problems. I will refer to this possible approach as a task variation policy. In effect, the vast majority of contemporary testing and examination systems adopt this approach *to some extent*. Perhaps the QCA was thinking more explicitly along these lines at one point in their guidance for Key Stage 2 Mathematics National Curriculum Tests. It recommended that teachers prepare children by practising in varying formats and contexts:

> Teachers need to... teach both informal and standard methods, using all four operations... to enable children to select appropriate strategies for questions presented in a variety of ways and situations. (QCA, 1998, p. 29)

I now explain a serious objection to strong versions of the task variation policy. It introduces an unacceptable element of luck if the assessment concerned is high stakes.

Suppose, then, that examiners took the 'teaching to the test' issue seriously and, with the best of intentions, introduced a substantial degree of variation from one test to the next 'equivalent' test. If this were done (and, as I say, it surely is the normal policy of those devising academic tests), candidates' scores would differ simply according to whether chance favoured them with question types with which they were familiar. Even if the most tough-minded and enlightened teachers resisted assessment pressure

---

[2]In England, each year there are attempts to produce national curriculum tests that are 'equivalent' to versions used on previous occasions, even though the questions for the new tests are different. This is done by means of piloting and sophisticated statistical manipulation. Such efforts have been severely criticized by researchers such as Tymms (2004). To my knowledge, no satisfactory response has been forthcoming from government agencies.

and continued to teach for understanding, their pupils would still be more proficient with known question types.

If these results contribute to a high-stakes accountability regime, then surely we should be very concerned about *significant* elements of chance in the results. (Empirical research also indicates that appreciable proportions of students taking National Curriculum tests will be the victim of 'misclassifications' even if reliability levels of 0.9 or above are achieved. This is held to be due in part to the fact that 'Any particular student may perform better or worse depending on the actual questions chosen for the particular administration of the test.' (Black and Wiliam, 2006, p. 120))

Does my argument here depend on an assumption that we can readily conceptualize 'types' of tasks, an assumption that I have sought to undermine earlier in my discussion? Am I being inconsistent? I do not think so, for the following reasons. The burden of my earlier line of reasoning is this: how tasks are categorized is not a matter that is independent of human meanings, practices and activities. The latter are complex and vary between cultures, within cultures and over time. Many of them undergo constant change. As a result, we are generally unable to make exact and detailed predictions about the degree of transfer between school performances such as test responses, and successful activity in everyday adult life. However, I emphasized that transfer does, of course, take place. Accordingly, I can grant that there will be more transfer between some kinds of teacher preparation and test performance than others, even though I will always find it very difficult to predict such transfer with any kind of precision. The existence of *varying* degrees of transfer is all that is needed for the argument about luck in test performance to go through.

Now, it must be acknowledged that, even in our ferociously high-stakes atmosphere, teachers and schools will not be condemned on the basis of one or two sets of results. All the same, each year a huge number of schools, teachers and pupils in England are involved in National Curriculum tests or GCSEs. So, there is a fair chance that *some* of them will be dogged by bad luck in the sense I have just explained.

Admittedly, in some subjects, and at some levels, the potential number of ways of asking candidates about the relevant knowledge is quite small. Thus, teachers could rehearse their pupils in all the variants, and the element of luck would be excluded. In other cases, there is apparently no limit to the number of possible task variants. Each year, inventive examiners committed to a variation policy could create something fresh. So, the performance of pupils with the 'same' knowledge could vary substantially, depending on the particular test they happen to take.

(It is often pointed out that if tests were longer and examiners were to take advantage of this to present a greater variety of tasks, then the element of luck would be reduced. The greater the variety of tasks candidates have to undertake, the greater the chance that all of them are confronted with a comparable mix of familiar and unfamiliar items. However, I would contend that in some subjects, tests would have to be extended to an unacceptable degree to reduce chance elements in this way. Cost and potential impact on students is likely to prevent this option being followed at a level that would make sufficient impact on the damaging elements of chance in the tests. The early history of National Curriculum Tasks stemming from the TGAT report sadly bears this out.)

Test designers committed to question variation policies could urge that I have missed the point. They could claim an enlightened view of proper educational objectives, and that they sought to encourage teachers to pursue these by varying question types from one year to the next. Their notion of a proper educational objective would include, or so they might urge, the kind of connectedness in knowledge and understanding that I have claimed is essential for adult functioning. (They might not characterize it in terms of 'connectedness', but this idea could be implicit in their thinking.) With the right variety of diet, and given effective teaching over a sufficient period, children would be able to succeed in anything that examiners might devise, or so my 'enlightened' test designers might maintain.

For example, in the first instance, pupils could add numbers presented horizontally, or add with counters, or add when given written problems involving the terms 'plus' or 'how many altogether'. The teacher would gently bombard the pupils with a range of addition tasks. The day would dawn when virtually any problem that involves addition regardless of format, presentation or context would be solved successfully by the pupils. Or so we might be told.

However, we have already seen some of the challenges posed by notions of similarity. We often cannot enjoy a high degree of confidence about the 'kinds' of things students can do. This is true even of a simple operation such as addition. Any belief to the contrary rests on types of convictions about transfer and appeals to fictitious mental traits so comprehensively criticized earlier.

Let me sum up the argument so far. We imagined what strategies might be devised to counter the traditional 'teaching to the test problem'. We saw that one obvious ploy, namely a task variation policy, would introduce an element of luck into the proceedings. If test results continue to be used to judge the effectiveness of teachers and schools in a high-stakes fashion, this chance component seems unfair and unethical, even if it only affects a small proportion of those concerned. If, on the other hand, the results are *not* part of an accountability system, then a degree of imperfection might be perfectly acceptable, depending, of course, on what other uses might be made of the assessment data.

Those unsympathetic to my critique as a whole will seize upon the tacit value judgements behind any kind of verdict that chance elements are unacceptable. If they feel that tests are the only proper way to hold education to account, then they may well draw the following conclusion: that the disadvantages of 'unfair' chance effects on given proportions of schools, teachers or students are outweighed by the advantages of a rigorous testing regime. So, two key questions to bear in mind as the discussion continues are: first – just how great are the 'costs' of high-stakes assessment? Second – are there any genuinely alternative strategies for holding education to account?

I turn from this to a concern about how both teachers and pupils actually view the nature of knowledge and understanding in an atmosphere in which teaching to the test is flourishing. At one time, it was fashionable to exhort teachers and pupils to be as explicit and as clear as possible about the knowledge and skills on which the lesson is focusing. Such guidance stemmed from the results of research into 'effective' teaching. For some years, it was a theme of Ofsted research reports and of school inspection reports. For instance: 'In the best lessons, learning objectives are explained to pupils and are used throughout to consolidate their progress; they are re-emphasised in the plenary session' (Ofsted, 2004, para 48). Or 'In the best lessons teachers make it clear to pupils what it is they are to learn...' (Ofsted, 1998b, p. 16).

Now, many teachers constrained by the pressures of league tables are likely to shift the emphasis of their teaching away from the promotion of properly understood knowledge, and towards developing in their students a limited range of performances identifiable in detail. The performances concerned will be those the teachers believe are the focus of tests. So, if the above-mentioned guidance were correct, teachers ought to maximize their chances of obtaining the intended learning outcomes by sharing those very objectives with their pupils.

However, this would transmit to students a powerful message about the fundamental character of learning. In this vision, to learn is to acquire a specific set of procedures, namely those required for success in the test. Yet, many school subjects cannot be translated into explicit test-related procedures without serious losses and distortions. Developing true understanding of academic content cannot be equated with polishing the performance of the A major scale for that Grade V Associated Board examination. Teachers being honest about the kind of learning they intend would, in effect, be indicating to children that they should not bother to try to 'understand'. Pupils would gather that they should ignore the challenge of developing properly connected knowledge and the applicability of such knowledge to a variety of circumstances. The authoritative message would be that they should concentrate instead on managing specified tasks in a restricted range of contexts.

Such a focus fails to reflect an adequate conception of knowledge, even if we judge knowledge worth having only according to what will help workers serving an industrial economy. For instance, to refer back to earlier discussion, mathematics teachers would be initiating their students into a thin rule-bound grasp of the subject. As a result, students often would be unable to make proper use of it in their lives, and might well develop and retain negative attitudes to the subject.

It is arguable that even within the academic curriculum, the effects will be less damaging in some areas than in others. Perhaps some aspects of foreign language programmes, for instance, *do* amount to a set of procedures of the kind that tests *can* probe effectively. In such cases, it may well be relatively straightforward to create classroom activities that have a readily identifiable and stable 'similarity' with the tasks featuring in the relevant tests. Hence, we can devote much curriculum time to acquiring the capacity to carry out such procedures. We can, in this sense, teach to the test without qualms and be perfectly clear with students that this is what we are doing. However, only a moment's reflection on the school curriculum reminds us that much of it does *not* resemble foreign language programmes in the crucial respects featured in this paragraph.

Of course, it will be argued that teachers should not seek to bypass understanding in favour of maximizing test results. Some urge that in fact they need not do this, because focusing on assessment for learning, whose objective is the promotion of rich or genuine knowledge and understanding, will actually contribute to the improvement of test scores (see, e.g., Wiliam, 2007, p. 1091). In response, we may concede the point, at least for the sake of argument, but still urge that the challenge of persuading teachers to see matters in this way, when under the pressure of high-stakes assessment, cannot be met in the current atmosphere. Teachers are only human.

To escape the serious problems rehearsed in this section, the assessment of pupil learning should not be used to hold schools and teachers to account. We need to develop other forms of accountability. I discuss these later.

Teaching to the test and assessment criteria

I show here that in a high-stakes assessment regime, interpretations of GCSE grading criteria, National Curriculum statements of attainment and the like will probably be confined to student achievements amenable to highly reliable judgements by a range of assessors. Features that conflict with this requirement will probably not be assessed. Teachers concentrate on what they know *will* be assessed.

Consider the following examples. I offer several, and many others could have been cited.

(Candidates) make an informed personal response to the author's ideas, opinions, and literary techniques ... (required for A grade in GCSE Classical Civilisation: QCA, 2007).

Candidates select and use an appropriate range of methods, sources, information and data to find out about issues or topics, building in critical evaluation when appropriate ... (Required for A grade in GCSE Health and Social Care: QCA, 2007).

(Candidates) will experiment with processes/techniques, materials/technologies, learning by experience to combine qualities effectively, and to take creative risks in developing connections between ideas, intentions and outcomes (Required for A grade in GCSE Applied Art and Design: QCA, 2007).

A noteworthy feature of these examples is the proliferation of expressions relating to *value* judgements, matters of interpretation and even aesthetic appreciation, such as 'informed personal response', 'creative risks' and 'critical evaluation'. How does the system ensure that these criteria are applied consistently by a range of markers? Generally, by 'training'. This will take a variety of forms, but it will invariably include sessions where, working together, examiners scrutinize pupil work and engage in whatever kinds of discussions are required to achieve consensus. It is a matter of common experience that over a period of time examiners can achieve a shared understanding of criteria associated with National Curriculum tests, GCSE examinations and so on. As a result, inter-marker reliability can improve significantly.

However, let us reflect for a moment on the criteria for appraising writing by candidates in AS and A2 English Literature, and in particular, ponder the use of expressions such as 'communicate content and meaning through expressive and accurate writing', and 'engage sensitively and with different readings and interpretations demonstrating clear understanding'. If it is insisted that they are amenable to consistent assessment by a range of markers, it is far from obvious that *all* the important aspects of writing are captured by such phrases. On the face of it, at least some of the features that require interpretation and aesthetic judgement resist a drive towards uniformity of judgement.

Three years ago, there was yet another public dispute about the marking of National Curriculum Tests. In this particular case, teachers objected to the assessment of the long writing elements of the Key Stage 2 English assessment, *on the grounds that it was not being marked consistently* (BBC, 2011). Many schools returned the scripts for a re-mark. Given the effect of these test results on the fate of schools, we can entirely understand teachers' reactions. Yet looked at in another way, a degree of inconsistency is to be expected from expert and conscientious markers seeking to appraise certain aspects of such a task. This story ended (happily?) with a government decision that the long writing task would be removed from Key Stage 2 externally marked National Curriculum English tests and be allocated to teachers to assess internally.

Similar issues arise with other sets of criteria. Consider the expression 'creative risk', from the Art and Design grade descriptions quoted above. One marker may feel very strongly that a student has taken a 'creative risk' that deserves every credit, while another's verdict might be that the student has gone too far and fails to understand that the impact of a design depends crucially on certain constraints. An examination system will be deemed effective if there are robust procedures for ironing out these inconsistencies. Yet, it is arguable that diverging verdicts should not *always* be regarded as a *problem*, a state of affairs which an effective assessment system *must* exclude. Markers who disagree might, nevertheless, be concerning themselves with important features of student work. These features will be sidelined in the drive for a reliable marking system. I am not encouraging inconsistency; this would be patently absurd. I am merely suggesting that there are strong reasons for objecting to an assessment system whose uses imply that inconsistency has to be viewed as inherently problematic. (Firestone, 1998, reported that the State of Vermont excluded poetry from student portfolios that formed an integral element in their assessment system, 'because it proved too hard to score reliably'. He added, 'Teachers feared that this decision would limit teaching of poetry' (p. 186)).

Some of the points just made are illuminated by the following activity, which I have tried with many groups of students and educational professionals at all levels over the last few years. Small groups are asked to write criteria which would enable 'markers' to grade apples on the four-point scale VERY GOOD APPLE, GOOD APPLE, SOUND APPLE WITH SOME WEAKNESSES AND FAILING APPLE. They invariably engage with the task enthusiastically in the first instance. Nevertheless, it is generally not long before they begin to look at me accusingly. 'But some people like crisp apples (or red apples, or a sharp taste etc.), and some don't.' 'It depends on the variety of apple!' 'Surely it's partly to do with what you are going to use the apples for – cooking apples like Bramleys are different – but then again the French sometimes use eating apples for tartelets' etc. I just nod sympathetically. If pushed, I say mildly 'Yes that was part of the point of the exercise really.' We then move on to write criteria for 'VERY GOOD PEAR', 'GOOD PEAR...' and so on. Unsurprisingly, similar protests arise. Pears are also 'interesting' because they do not remain at any one grade for very long, as pear lovers know only too well. Finally, the killer activity is to attempt the construction of *generic* criteria which would apply to apples *and* pears – or perhaps a wider range of fruit. 'But this is impossible – our descriptions are so bland as to be virtually meaningless.' 'But we're squeezing out the different value judgments made about particular fruits.' 'But we're having to introduce norm-referenced descriptions of how people react. Here's what we've got so far: VERY GOOD FRUIT – fruit which most people find the most enjoyable to eat. GOOD FRUIT – fruit which people find enjoyable to eat but the enjoyment is less intense than that provoked by the top graded fruit.' And so on. Proper descriptions and evaluations of specific fruit cannot figure at all. (One group of students 'solved' the problem by using the criterion 'fit for purpose'.)

I suggest that important lessons can be drawn from these activities for the fate of any assessment criteria incorporating value judgements. Elsewhere (Davis, 2010), I have suggested that in the context of grading fruit, if we sought consistency of judgements across a range of fruit graders, we would have to invent an authority called 'Ofgrub' to lay down the fruit values that must inform the graders' verdicts. But just how is Ofgrub's choice of values to be justified? In the case of assessment judgements in education, whose judgements are to achieve currency, and why? Equally, expert examiners in the Arts and humanities will not, if left to themselves, agree about everything. I am worried about the consequences if we try to make them feel that they *ought* to agree with each other whenever their judgements are properly based on their expertise.

Moreover, readily identifiable signs of the 'presence' of value-laden features such as elegance or creative risk will need to be explicitly embedded in the assessment criteria to secure consistency of judgements. Teachers will become aware of these signs and are likely to teach students to include them in their work without regard to whether those students are seeking the real qualities of elegance or creative risk.

The 'backwash' of high-stakes testing is an acknowledged phenomenon. If some features of student achievement cannot be assessed reliably by different markers, then they will not be assessed. Teachers will know that they are not, and their approaches to teaching and the curriculum will be influenced accordingly.[3]

Art and Music often lack prominence in the assessment for accountability portfolio. This is certainly true in England. We may have mixed feelings about this. If these subjects featured strongly in our accountability regime, then more time and resources might be devoted to them in comparison with the 'basics' than is currently the case. However, their assessment would then need to aspire to high levels of consistency. The arguments above suggest that there could be serious costs. It is far from obvious that those aspects of the arts that can be assessed reliably are the only ones that really matter in educational terms.

Accountability and the 'added-value' approach

Test and examination performance is known to be correlated with the socio-economic status of the pupils. Other factors over which schools have no control also seem to be important in test

---

[3]Empirical research supports this claim – see Harlen (2004) in a research review of a large number of studies.

performance. Over the last decade or so, there have been attempts to discount such effects. Efforts have been made to measure how well schools are doing in terms of the *progress* made by their pupils. This approach has been accorded a lower profile in the United Kingdom, at least for now. The Coalition government has decided that league tables based on added-value measures will not be issued for the time being. However, it is by no means certain that added-value ideas will not resume their high profile at some point, so I develop a brief critique of them in this section.

In England from 2003, primary school value-added tables were published that took into account schools' results at the end of Key Stage 1, together with performance achieved at the end of Key Stage 2. The rationale for this practice went as follows. It was possible to discover what pupils knew at the age of 6–7, and when they were about to leave school at 11. This provided a measure of progress over four years. Taking account of background features which might influence performance, using indicators such as the number of children on free school meals, we could judge how much a school is doing for its pupils in comparison with other schools teaching similar pupils. Of course, according to the resulting statistical tables, the progress of pupils in some schools would be 'above average' while in others it would be 'below average'. Value-added tables for secondary schools in England based on related principles existed before 2003.

Attempts to produce performance indicators relating to pupil progress arguably represented well-intentioned departures from the use of crude results to judge the worth of schools. Yet, there were serious problems. The notion of 'similarity' was at the heart of some of the difficulties. Common sense suggests several aspects of a school's catchment likely to affect how readily the pupils will learn. These aspects will include whether the children are cold and hungry at home, have enough sleep, how much conversation they have with their parents and the level of their parents' education. So, we could try to compare the progress of a particular set of pupils with lots of other sets of pupils at schools where the above factors correspond closely. The trouble is that we simply do not know about all the factors, external to schools themselves, that may affect learning progress and, hence, cannot control for them when we try to make comparisons. Such factors may be complex and unstable. Possibilities not always considered include subtle environmental pollution effects, or cultural factors specific to an area that are not identified by superficial attributions of socio-economic status.

Note also that intricate, elusive and ephemeral forces might affect performance at the end of Key Stage 1. For instance, some 'middle-class' parents may prepare children for their first school assessment hurdles. Yet, they may not even be aware they are doing this, and some parents belonging to this social category may not be doing it at all. It could relate to aspects of conversation and play, shared by child and parent. There might be no way of identifying which parents offer the richer stimulation concerned. The nature of the resulting challenge for the school seeking to add value is not easy to predict. It seems that it could either make it harder or easier! On the one hand, some children might be given a flying start by their parents. Hence, they might progress more quickly than apparently similar children in other schools. So, their school would unfairly be given extra credit. On the other hand, it might actually be more difficult for their school to be seen to add value, given the quality of the extra-school input and the resulting impressive Key Stage 1 results. To repeat, we know too little, and this ignorance does not seem to be a temporary difficulty.

Added-value experts recognize that there will be chance variations between the progress of apparently comparable cohorts of pupils, and that these variations must be added to the built-in error that any test will have, however cleverly designed. So, schools would have to be scrutinized in value-added terms over several years for more robust judgements to be made about their effectiveness. Yet, much may change about a school over time. Some staff may leave, and others join. The head might be replaced. Individual teachers will vary in their energy, motivation and competence from year to year. Some schools have significant proportions of pupils who join them from elsewhere and only stay for a short period. We may be forgiven for wondering what precisely is meant by 'the same school' when it is considered over periods of several years. In the light of this, we may begin to wonder about the nature of that which is being held responsible when we insist that schools should be accountable for the 'quality' of their provision.

Note yet another problem about 'value-added'. Its defenders assume that we can simply appeal to common sense, in order to choose exit assessments that probe the *same knowledge or subject matter* as that dealt with by assessments encountered by the younger pupils. For instance, some Key Stage 1 tests are supposed to measure pupils' mathematical achievements. At eleven, a battery of tests are taken, some of which are again devoted to 'mathematics'. From the value-added perspective, we should now have the necessary information to enable us to detect how far the children have travelled in mathematics between the ages of 6–7 and 11. Hence, on the account under consideration, we can judge the quality of a given school by comparing its pupils' mathematical progress with 'similar' pupils in other schools.

Yet, it is not obvious which mathematics test should be used for eleven year olds to measure their progress. The school might believe that it is adding to the 'mathematics value' that the pupils demonstrated on entry to Key Stage 2. Yet, this could be missed by the allegedly relevant exit tests. Were a subtly different mathematics exit test to be employed, our school might be 'shown' to be doing better in comparison with equivalent institutions. Or worse! Yet, both of the potential tests may appear to be measuring the 'same thing', namely mathematics.

To sum up, robust and definitive reasons for selecting one particular exit test rather than another as part of a value-added measure are simply not available. Yet, National Curriculum Tests and public examinations were integral features of value-added measures. The choices were made and were marketed as though there were no trace of the arbitrary about them. We should note in passing that from 2016 English four and five year olds will be subjected to compulsory tests in basic subject areas, and policy makers justify this by referring to measuring the progress of children during the primary school stage.

I conclude that the present Coalition government's decision to abandon league tables based on added-value approaches was a move in the right direction, though their motives are questionable. It is important to note that giving test data to schools themselves about how they compare with apparently similar schools, a policy pursued by projects such as ALIS and PIPs,[4] is a very different matter. Schools could be aware of the fallibility of the available information but still make sensitive use of it in their own particular contexts. If cost permitted, data could be offered on schools' value-added measures according to several different exit tests and teachers could weigh for themselves the relevance of the potentially conflicting results.

The problem with holding teachers to account for their methods

In the last few decades, UK governments have been increasingly prescriptive about teaching methods and approaches. This has been especially apparent in the primary sector. The National Literacy and Numeracy Strategies provided ideal lesson structures, recommended proportions of whole class teaching and even detailed how phonics should be delivered.

These recent levels of intervention were quite unprecedented. In the early days of the National Curriculum, ministers took a pride in asserting that although Government was now in the 'secret garden' of the curriculum legislating about what should be taught, they were (of course) leaving it to the professionals to decide how to teach. In later developments, influenced by the effective teacher and effective schools' research programme, some came to believe that there was evidence showing specific teaching approaches to be the most effective and that this justified prescribing teaching methods. Apparently, we were in possession of a 'technology of teaching'.

Some educators objected to teachers being treated as mere technicians. It was believed that teachers should be viewed as

---

[4]ALIS (Advanced Level Information System), PIPs (Performance Indicators in Primary Schools) YELLIS (Year 11 Information System) and other information systems are based at the Curriculum, Evaluation and Management Centre, Durham University, UK. They offer schools data about how their pupils' performance compares with that of similar pupils in similar schools.

professionals who should make their own decisions. However, this attitude did not cut much ice with policy makers eager to raise standards. They presumably felt that if we knew what works in the classroom, then we really ought to teach accordingly and not allow ourselves to become precious about teachers' dignity and status.

Government is currently moving away from prescription. This policy change is made explicit in recent modifications to the Framework for School Inspections. For instance, 'Inspectors must not give the impression that Ofsted favours a particular teaching style' (Ofsted, 2014).

However, some approaches such as systematic phonics are still strongly favoured, so it is worth reflecting on the problems inherent in any attempts by the state to intervene in teaching methods.

Examples of methods that were prescribed included the following: divide children into sets by attainment; teach phonics in a specific way; and bring children together at the end of a lesson for a plenary session in which themes arising from the body of the lesson are drawn together and consolidated.

Much of this may seem perfectly acceptable at first sight. However, to the extent that teachers were being forced to adopt official methods, they should not have been held responsible for the results. Instead, the designers of the National Literacy and Numeracy Strategies, for example, should have been blamed if pupil learning outcomes did not reach 'expected levels'. Equally, if results had been splendid, then the method creators should have received every credit. (Though if 'results' simply meant improved performance in public tests and examinations, then we should not have become too excited in either case, as I argued earlier.)

Further, when we look closer at least *some* of the attempts to prescribe teaching methods, additional problems emerge. Effective teaching, whether in the course of interaction with the whole class or smaller groups, seems bound to take account of the pupils' responses. I mean both that it *ought* to take account of responses, and also that in practical terms *it is impossible not to in any case*. This means that any particular lesson is to a degree unpredictable, even if a detailed plan is being used, such as one informed by government stress on phonics.

The teacher has to gauge minute by minute the level of her students' interest and motivation and the extent to which they seem to be gaining understanding. She continually modifies her style of explanation, tone, timing and organization. That is why one teacher's lesson on a particular topic may differ significantly from another's, even if the same content and similar age and attainment groupings of pupils are involved.

Suppose, for instance, that teachers were required to explain a concept in mathematics or science according to a specific prescription. This might take the form of a text, devised by experts in the subjects, that the teacher had to use. They might read it from a copy, or feel that it would be better if delivered directly, so they could learn it off by heart before the lesson. It is very difficult to take such a suggestion seriously. Any teacher worth even a fraction of her salary would note the reactions of her students after the first sentence or so. She might take questions, amplify what she had just said or even move on very quickly to a later section if she realizes that elements of the official explanation are excessively familiar and easy for her students. If we videoed ten teachers allegedly implementing the prescribed explanation, we would see ten different complex social events.

If the teacher did not enter into dynamic interaction with her students, would she actually be teaching? If teachers paid no attention to how their students responded to their actions, they could be replaced by pre-recorded teacher speeches or pre-recorded teacher demonstrations. Clearly *this* could be prescribed for schools by an authoritative agency. It might be characterized as a 'teacher-proof' method. Some politicians place so little trust in teachers that they would be delighted to find a way of embedding such methods in schools.

Prescriptions could take other guises. Perhaps certain questions could be laid down, or the use of specific items of equipment insisted upon. Again, we will wonder whether, once we take account of the myriads of micro-decisions made by teachers in the course of the lesson, we still have an identifiable approach whose success in promoting learning could possibly be supported by research evidence. There will often be nothing in these educational contexts to correspond with, say, the drugs that are legitimately and rigorously tested by means of randomized-controlled trials.

The supporter of prescriptions might try once more to make her case. The trouble with the argument so far, she might urge, is that the target approaches are absurdly narrow and specific. Instead, we should be talking about broader categories of teaching. What broader categories might our prescriber have in mind? They might include 'chalk and talk', 'group work', 'interactive teaching', 'lecture', 'student-centred workshop' and many other approaches. By their very nature, each of these categories covers a huge range of possibilities. In order for research to support their effectiveness, there would have to be at least one feature in common to all the examples subsumed in any one category, and it would have to be a feature on whose presence in a teaching episode a range of impartial observers could agree. Such a feature could not, for instance, be a complex social phenomenon open to a range of interpretations. It would have to be something specific and observable. So, for example, a 'lecture' might have to be identified by the fact that the tutor was standing at the front of the class, talking without interruption for, say not less than 80 per cent of the time and so forth. We are being driven back to the specific, and, arguably, to aspects of lessons that no professional teacher could afford to follow in a rigid and literal-minded fashion.

Moreover, even where it makes any kind of sense to think of 'methods', teachers may need to switch from one method to another as a result of her appraisals of student reactions. Consider, for instance, a typical sequence of events in an English comprehensive school. Initially, a teacher decides that an open-ended interactive discussion approach is appropriate for the treatment of a certain PSE issue. As the lesson develops, however, the students may become overexcited or 'silly', so she quickly modifies her style in the direction of a more structured lesson with an emphasis on her authority from the front. In extreme circumstances, teachers may need to abandon a lesson completely and begin on something else. If someone was incapable of exercising this level of professional autonomy, many would be unable to regard them as worthy of the name 'teacher'.

I have argued elsewhere (Davis, 2012, 2013) that there are some specific problems with synthetic phonics per se that mean it is wholly inappropriate as a prescription for approaches to teaching early reading. The universal phonics 'check' for five year olds is followed by a retake in Year 2 for pupils who 'fail' the first one; in many respects, these 'checks' are high stakes, with an inevitable 'backwash' on the pedagogies prioritized by teachers when dealing with early reading.

Ofsted cannot detect whether schools cause pupils to learn

Large claims have always been made for Ofsted inspections.

> The published inspection report tells parents, the school and the wider community about the quality of education at the school and whether pupils achieve as much as they can (Ofsted, 2005 p. 4).

Now, it is obvious that *some* features of a school or a teaching situation can be readily detected by an outside observer, even on the basis of relatively brief inspection. Some of these have been referred to as compliance issues. Does the school obey Health and Safety regulations? Is the school coming together for an act of worship each day? Is there a Child Protection Policy? Does the school have up-to-date policies for the various subjects? What proportion of the teaching time is allocated to each of the curriculum areas? There are also factual points to which the school can provide straightforward answers for inspectors. These include patterns of school attendance, performance on compulsory national tests, school accommodation, staffing and so on. Moreover, dramatically negative situations could be identified on the basis of brief observations. The school might be closed when it was supposed to be open. It could be filthy, or even in a state of dangerous disorder.

Ofsted inspection verdicts cover many of these aspects of schools and classrooms. Arguably, external checks on these can be very helpful. However, official verdicts also encompass rather different issues relating to the role of schools in bringing about learning. The challenge for inspectors is to convince us that their judgements about the quality of school provision are worthy of respect. School reports are riddled with confident pronouncements of this kind. Inspectors are asked to evaluate 'how well teaching and/or training and resources promote learning...' (Ofsted, 2007, p. 19). When inspectors judge that teaching and learning is 'very good', they have reached the conclusion that 'Teaching methods are well selected...' (Ofsted, 2003, p. 62). Note some characteristically self-assured Ofsted examples of judgements about teaching quality. 'The teaching was excellent in every aspect but particularly the pace and clarity of the explanations, the precise focus of the lesson's objectives and the use of support staff, including the computer technician, to support slower learners' (Ofsted, 2005a, p. 13). And 'Pupils' knowledge, progress in the lesson and attainment is very high and above national expectations for this age. This can be accredited to the exemplary teaching the pupils experience over time and the very high expectations of all staff' (Ofsted, 2005b, p. 5).

The average Ofsted inspector is an experienced professional, with knowledge of the age groups concerned and accustomed to observing teaching. Moreover, as Ofsted inspection guidelines indicate, the available evidence extends well beyond the simple observation of a few lessons. Inspectors can investigate student work, question pupils and staff, scrutinize the long-term planning in which the observed lessons are embedded and compare pupils' current written work with that being produced at the beginning of that academic year or at some other useful point in time. They can track school processes such as evaluation and performance management.

Yet, none of this goes anywhere near to justifying verdicts on school quality based on the extent to which schools bring about learning. There are at least two formidable challenges. The first concerns the possibility of detecting the development of real knowledge on the basis of limited evidence. The second is about whether, even if such learning could be uncovered, inspectors could ever be in a position to judge that the school is playing a significant role in bringing about that learning.

Turning to the first challenge, if schools aspire to develop children's 'connected' understanding, their contribution cannot be assessed adequately by means of the limited evidence available to the most perceptive of inspectors. It would be difficult even to check whether just one pupil had learned in this rich fashion as a result of the data gathered during an inspection. Teachers begin to reach tentative judgements about these kinds of achievements on the basis of dynamic interactions with pupils over periods of *months*, not days.

In the case of younger children learning abstract subjects such as mathematics and science, 'connected' knowledge grows slowly and erratically. It is often inappropriate, either for teachers or for schools more generally, to think in terms of specific elements of knowledge which children will obtain in the short term. Inspectors certainly should not assume that most lessons contribute to learning in a way that fits this short-term paradigm. If schools insisted on thinking in this fashion, perhaps because of perceived pressure from Ofsted, the effect would be to distort the intended learning in the direction of narrowly conceived skills or of the acquisition of barely understood 'facts' which could be quickly taught and which the children could only exercise in the kinds of contexts in which they were acquired. As we saw earlier, this is not the kind of knowledge that has clear and specific relationships with the qualities they will ultimately require as contributors to a competitive industrial economy.

I suggest that Ofsted's real approach differs dramatically from that suggested by its rhetoric. They appreciate the points I have just made, even if such appreciation only extends to a subliminal awareness in many cases. They know that what they actually do, for the most part, is to discover whether schools are using 'appropriate' approaches. They think that *these* can be discovered on the basis of limited observation, and they have already decided which methods *in general* are effective.

It may be objected that even if this has been true in the past, it is not the case now. We have already noted that the latest Inspection Framework insists that inspectors must refrain from giving the impression that Ofsted favours any particular teaching style. However, if this injunction is taken to heart, we may wonder just how judgements can be consistent from one inspector to another. I suspect that inspectors' approval of certain approaches to teaching and learning will become tacit; this will replace the explicit guidance to be found in past Inspection Frameworks. The approved approaches will still be present in some sense, for if they are not, a reasonable level of consistency in judgements will be impossible.

Again, it may be objected that this applies, if at all, to past practice. It is no longer relevant since, at the time of writing (2014), Ofsted has ceased grading teachers on individual lessons. My response to this point is that even if individual lessons are not graded, it surely will remain the case that verdicts on the teaching seen by inspectors contribute to the overall judgements of the school inspection concerned.

I also suggest that schools will attempt to anticipate which teaching approaches are 'approved', despite the new wording of the Framework, and despite the fact that individual lessons are no longer awarded grades. Accordingly, schools will seek to 'show' these approaches during an inspection, given the current power relationships between schools and Ofsted. The 'showing' will be an attempt to make visible something which cannot be made visible and, hence, may prove destructive of the school's true qualities.

This finally brings us to a consideration of the second challenge confronting inspectors – the issue of the actual causes of learning. It is difficult enough for experienced heads, steering schools over periods of years or so, to know how far particular approaches are responsible for children's learning (if we briefly put to one side the doubts about identifying approaches per se). If it makes sense to speak of the causes of learning at all, then we are dealing with an extremely complex set of interacting influences. The latter include short-term triggers, together with factors that take a long time to bring about their effects. As we noted above, abstract concepts such as place value in mathematics, force in science or the notion of a sentence will take years to develop. Many teachers will play a part in their growth, as will factors outside the school gates. The students on whom the causes are supposed to operate differ from each other at any one time in respect of cognitive states, motivation and in many other ways.

Furthermore, establishing that schools are causing the children to learn would not be sufficient. Even if this could be demonstrated, which it could not, the inspector would also need to be clear from the evidence that in some sense schools *intended* the learning concerned to develop as a result of their particular approaches, approaches which schools had consciously adopted and sought to maintain. Inspection should not hold schools responsible for 'lucky' successes. The whole point of accountability is to hold agents and agencies responsible for choices that they themselves have made.

How should we hold schools and teachers to account?

Some policy makers will dismiss my negative arguments. 'You are unrealistic!' they will complain. 'Our current accountability process may be far from perfect, but it is the best we can do. Education is far too important to be left to its practitioners. They *must* be held to account. What could possibly replace accountability through assessment?'

There is no easy answer. This is partly because the advantages of any candidate accountability system should not be judged on their own when we make policy decisions. Instead, their strengths should be weighed against their potential costs both to individuals and to society as a whole. The costs of our current practices are heavy and very obvious to most working in the school system. I do not refer to financial costs in particular, though these are not inconsiderable. I am talking rather about the *educational* damage to schools and their students.

There are genuine alternatives to current policy. Consider the specific question of making schools accountable. The distorting effects of a high-stakes regimen stem from the inappropriate relationship between those defending their practices – schools and teachers, and those to whom accounts are being rendered. The latter is constituted by the state and its agencies such as Ofsted, together with a public whose perceptions are to a degree constructed and tainted by the whole idea of league tables and broader aspects of the 'audit culture' in which we now live.

Many have pointed to the destructive effects of the audit culture and the disappearance of *trust*. If policy makers could rethink the relationship between educators and the state so that trust was renewed, this could transform the effects of accountability. Needless to say, I am *not* advocating trust to be interpreted as a blind faith in the infallibility of teachers when educating their students on behalf of society. On the contrary, trust may be characterized broadly as an attitude of *respect* for the expertise of the professional, combined with the legitimate expectation that the professional will be prepared and even enthusiastic about explaining and justifying practice to external auditors.

Even sympathetic readers may be pessimistic about the chances that trust could ever be reinstated. If anything, the obsession with performance indicators combined with low levels of trust are examples of phenomena that will become even more firmly ensconced in our society in the next decade or so. Or so many may feel. My only response can be that if enough people understood the pointlessness and destructiveness of all this, then their perceptions might finally have an impact on relevant political decisions.

If it is accepted that test results, even in their allegedly more sophisticated versions as added-value scores, should no longer dominate accountability processes, inspection can still play an important role. However, the relationship between inspectors and educators must change. There needs to be a *genuine* dialogue between two partners in the educational enterprise. The inspectors should not act as a dominant partner, but as external professionals who can both contribute to the business of the educational institution and learn from it. They should not bring to their scrutiny of teaching and leadership preconceived ideas about 'good practice' derived from supposed expertise in 'what works' – the non-existent and, indeed, frequently conceptually impossible 'technologies' of effective schooling and effective teaching. In contrast, they ought to offer wide professional understanding of an extensive repertoire of approaches and a deep appreciation of the complex reasons for making specific selections from this repertoire in particular contexts. The fact that inspectors are not supposed to give the impression that they favour particular approaches may appear to be a policy change representing a step in the right direction. However, I am not holding my breath, particularly as there is no sign whatever that the power relationship between inspectors and those inspected is improving.

Incidentally, at the end of an Ofsted visit, the relevant educational institution should be allowed to produce a report on the inspectors. This report should have official standing. Its significance should rank with the Ofsted report. As with the inspectors' verdicts, such reports would of course need to be backed up with detailed evidence. Schools issuing critical accounts of their inspection without proper justification would, by their very actions, be exposing their own weakness. That would be one way in which a healthy *mutual* accountability would be maintained.

If quality is no longer defined directly in terms that incorporate pupil learning outcomes, it needs an alternative interpretation. Issues of *compliance* can still feature – a school cannot offer high-quality provision if it falls down on these. Health and Safety measures must be in place, the school must, among other things, be addressing the subject content laid down in the National Curriculum and so on. I suggest that, in addition, quality should be understood as having at its very heart matters of value or principle. These value issues ultimately would be defended by an appeal to fundamental educational aims. Needless to say, it should not be left to teachers and other education professionals to determine these. Similarly, it is not the exclusive prerogative of doctors to decide the values underlying the prioritizing of scarce NHS resources. Ultimately, our pluralist society must reach a democratic verdict here.

However, I have now reached a point in this book where I allow myself to take account of values that transcend mere instrumental aims for education, hoping that others in our liberal democracy might agree. (See White, 2007, for a proper examination of educational aims.) In this spirit, I suggest some desirable features of learning contexts which could be sought by inspectors. In listing these features, I am not for a moment suggesting that they are not already seen as important both by schools and those to whom they are accountable. Yet, while our high-stakes system continues, it can never flourish as much as it should at the heart of the educational process.

Are students gaining experience of working together? Do these experiences involve the pupils in valuing each other's contributions and respecting individual differences in terms of culture and religion? Are they encouraged to understand what they are being taught, rather than simply to absorb it and memorize it? Are pupils invited to question and to examine critically material offered by teachers? Are they provoked to develop intellectual curiosity and do they have opportunities to follow up their curiosity with teacher's support? Are they being introduced to a range of ideas and of subjects to whet their appetite for more? Are the pupils for the most part enjoying their learning? Relationships in schools, between staff and pupils, and between the various adults within the institution, can also be scrutinized with reference to key values. Questions that can be addressed include the following. Are managers treating staff with respect? Is there genuine consultation when policy issues are decided? Do teaching staff treat children with respect? Are school rules reviewed regularly in consultation with staff, pupils and parents? What is the quality of the partnership between School Governors and School Staff? Is the school discipline policy implemented fairly and effectively?

Either Ofsted inspectors or old-style HMI can discover, in broad terms, whether schools and other educational institutions are at least trying to work in accordance with such principles. The kind of evidence required, and the judgements that would result, should not come up against the basic limitations of inspection of schools as learning producers discussed earlier. Pinpoint accuracy of interpretation and judgement should not be necessary or even relevant. Inspectors can discuss with the institution under scrutiny its ongoing evaluations of attempts to incorporate the values in question. They would not be seeking to 'measure' the evaluations, but rather to engage with them and hope to contribute to their improvement. This version of accountability is far from being neat and tidy. Yet, it could be fair to the teachers and pupils concerned. It could play a crucial role in raising standards which were about true educational quality rather than the achievement of performance indicators.

Many have advocated the virtues of institutional self-evaluation, and up to recently, Ofsted inspection arrangements officially incorporated this element. Schools and colleges were supposed to develop systems of self-review in which they regularly and rigorously judged their own progress and performance against self-imposed targets. They had to be prepared to explain and demonstrate their self-review systems and processes to outside agencies. While the role of institutional self-evaluation in school inspection has been put on the back burner for the time being, it may return in some guise, so, I now offer some comments and reflections about this.

The focus on self-evaluation in inspections may have seemed encouraging at the time. However, was the multifaceted and context-related character of 'improvement' truly understood by those holding educational institutions to account? Certainly, society through its agencies including the Inspectorate has every right to influence the values and aims to which educational institutions aspire. Nevertheless, the guidance for self-review concentrated heavily on 'data' which largely consists of test results. The 'issues' that schools were encouraged to highlight in their self-evaluation reports and the 'evidence' they were supposed to offer were dominated by tests. Notions of 'progress' were similarly referenced to test results.

Failing a more radical alteration in the power balance between schools and the Inspectorate, even self-review itself would continue to be subject to the familiar distorting effects of our audit culture. Educators would still feel that they were obliged to implement the 'right' self-evaluation moves and to ensure that these are 'seen' by inspectors. They would calculate which visible symptoms of self-evaluation will be sought by inspectors, and put their energies into ensuring that these symptoms are manifest in all their practices.

This represents a destructive alternative to what many educators would urge could be a profoundly important option for educational accountability, namely genuine and deep self-evaluation on the part of teachers, schools and other educational institutions in conjunction with external auditors who properly understand the professional challenges, complexities and values concerned.

Conclusion

Assessment has many important functions. One purpose dominates in contemporary educational life in many countries, namely that of holding educational institutions and their teachers to account. I have shown that, in principle, there can be no basis for claims about a detailed and specifiable relationship between test preparation and test performance, on the one hand, and adults' contributions in their role as employees to modern industrial economies, on the other. I went on to explore the incompatibilities between certain kinds of 'teaching to the test' and the development of the kind of knowledge and understanding needed by adults in contemporary society.

Hence, I argued, the content and delivery of the curriculum should not be dominated by the perceived requirements of tests. There are alternative constructive approaches to holding education to account. However, these require a very different way of thinking about the relationship between educational institutions and the State from that currently dominating the scene.

Part Two

The Nature and Purpose of Educational Assessment – A Response to Andrew Davis

Christopher Winch

Introduction

In this response, I set out my own views on the nature and purposes of assessment practices, noting points of agreement and disagreement with Andrew Davis. My starting point is to look at assessment as an important aspect of educational practices, indicate the variety of different purposes for which assessment is used and show the degree to which these different purposes can be reliably realized. I also comment on whether or not certain purposes for which assessment is used are worthwhile. I devote considerable attention, both to 'high-stakes' assessment and to assessment for professional purposes. Although I maintain that the latter is an aspect of the former, I also believe that it raises distinct issues that need to be kept separate from other aspects of high-stakes assessment.

Practices of assessment

The concept of assessment belongs with a number of other central concepts that we need in order to understand education, including *values, aims, curriculum* and *pedagogy*. Why is this? If we accept that education is a purposive activity which is undertaken seriously (i.e. primarily as the preparation of the young for a worthwhile life), then those who educate will desire to know how successful they are. If they are not so concerned, then we might wish to say that they are not serious about educating, and are only apparently doing so, 'going through the motions' as it were, just as one can *seem* to plan an activity, seem to communicate and seem to control what one is doing, without *actually* doing so. We could say that the realm of concern with success in education is the realm in which the concept of assessment holds most sway.

However, no easy definition of assessment is possible, but we can identify a range of practices that fall within the classification of 'assessment' in modern educational practice. Broadly speaking, educational assessment is concerned with whether or not, and maybe to what degree, the intentions of an educational activity have been fulfilled. But this may be done for a variety of reasons, more or less related to each other. Some are for accountability purposes, others not. Assessment and accountability are two related but distinct concepts. Accountability is concerned with whether or not a delegated agent has carried out tasks for which he has been given authority and resources and, possibly, for how well that agent has carried out that task and with what degree of prudence resources dedicated to it have been expended. The moral principle here is reciprocal obligation undertaken either contractually or informally. For educational institutions, some form of assessment of how successfully the intentions of educational activities have been fulfilled is almost invariably a key instrument in establishing accountability, since accountability is concerned with the success of educational activities towards which resources have been directed.

Accountability and assessment

It is important to state the general moral nature of accountability requirements because they are too easily confused with preoccupations of the day, or with the perspective that a certain kind of economist brings to bear on such issues. Foremost amongst these is the 'Agent–Principal' problem often cited by economists. A Principal P gives an agent A resources to carry out task T. The problem is, how does P ensure that the objectives of A are solely focused on the carrying out of T? After all, A may not care about T or even be opposed to carrying it out if it involves too much 'disutility' for himself? The problem thus becomes one of 'incentivizing' A to carry out P's wishes, namely carrying out T, when P cannot trust A to do so. In these circumstances, it is natural to find a proxy for success in carrying out T which A will aim for. So, the reward for carrying out T or the punishment for failing to do so (call it I) becomes the incentive to carry out T and thus the *motivation* for A to do so. But, then, A is motivated to acquire I rather than to carry out T and, unless the acquisition of I and the carrying out of T (just as the Principal intended) are closely aligned, the danger of unintended and unwelcome consequences for P are always present. One of several problems with this approach, noted by le Grand (2003), is that one can destroy certain forms of altruistic motivation through such an incentive structure. If A wants to carry out T because he believes in the value of T, but is rewarded or punished by the threat or promise of I, then he will tend to be motivated by I because of the drastic personal consequences of failing to carry out T. But carrying out T is no longer the primary motivation, the acquisition of I is. The complication is made greater because, in order to ensure that a very complex task like educating someone is actually carried out (the T in question in this case), one needs some kind of measurable proxy for success, G such as achievement data. So, actually the incentive I (the motivation to carry out T) is awarded as a result of achievement of a good G, a proxy indicator for carrying out T. It follows that the Agent A is motivated by I to deliver G, rather than to carry out T as originally envisaged. The agent's motivation is thus two removes from the aim of the activity. T is replaced by G and motivation to deliver G is secured by I.

But, we do not have to enter the often bizarre world of Agent and Principal in order to understand the basic idea of accountability. If someone agrees to carry out something in return for resources to do so, then the basic idea of reciprocal obligation and hence mutual trust is engendered, or so most people assume if they have not been seduced by the assumptions of economists' models of utility maximization. Does that mean that accountability need not be an issue for education? Unfortunately not, because although educators are thankfully not in the vast majority of cases the dessicated utility-maximisers of economic theory, they are not endowed either with perfect knowledge, perfect expertise or completely pure and unsullied motivations – they are human. Sometimes, indeed, they may consider that their own personal code of ethics is affronted by what they are asked to do as part of the accountability relationship. This may lead to painful personal dilemmas and to compromise in the extent to which they can fully implement their own personal values. This in turn may lead to obedience rather than active consent in carrying out their duties. These are all features of the human condition which the designers and administrators of educational institutions, whether they are public or private, must take into account in governance. And there are often no easy solutions. So, we need to take accountability seriously whether we are talking in the terms preferred by economists or not and whether we are talking of private or public educational institutions. It is to be expected that there will be difficulties and conflicts in doing so. Does that mean we should give up on accountability? If it is at bottom a simple and fundamental ethical relationship, then the answer must be 'no'. Here, as in most other areas of human life, complete harmony between participants is not possible.

The purposes of assessment

Having established the general outlines of the accountability–assessment relationship, we can now consider the various main purposes for which assessment practices exist. These are the major reasons why assessment is carried out in modern education systems. The list may not be exhaustive but it covers the major cases.

(a) Establishing whether and how an individual has learned what it is intended that he has learned with a view to assisting him in his learning (sometimes called 'formative assessment').

It is arguable that this is the most fundamental of the possible forms of assessment, because, as Flew (1976) argued, it is an indicator of the seriousness with which a teacher approaches teaching and hence whether or not he is teaching in any significant sense at all. The thinking goes along these lines.

1   Teaching is a purposive activity whose aim is to enable pupils to learn what the teacher intends them to learn.

2   If one is serious about one's intention, one will take steps to ensure that one's actions realize that intention.

3   Teachers need to be serious about ensuring that their purpose in enabling pupils to learn is realized, by taking appropriate measures to do so.

4   These measures will necessarily involve inspecting whether or not pupils have learned what the teacher intended that they should learn. This is formative assessment.

5   Therefore anyone engaged in teaching (as opposed to merely appearing to do so) will take steps to assess whether pupils have learned what it is intended that they should learn.
(a slightly expanded version of the argument in Flew, 1976, pp. 88–94, esp. p. 89)

A couple of points are in order at this stage. First, that teaching is usually a cyclical activity. One lesson ends and the next lesson takes over where the previous one finished. So, the point of teacher assessment is not merely to ascertain whether his aims have been achieved, but also to adjust his plans for the following lesson in the light of what has been accomplished in the first. On this perspective, this kind of assessment is a critical point within an extended teaching cycle. Second, by carrying out an assessment of a pupil's achievement, a teacher should be trying to ascertain what the pupil finds difficult or easy and to gain some insight into how such difficulties, if they exist, may be removed on a future occasion or how the level of challenge can be enhanced. Such an exercise will require diagnostic skills, together with an insight into how the pupil learns (and fails to learn).

The ability to carry out formative assessment in the above sense may look like an obvious attribute that teachers should possess in abundance as a result of their professional preparation. It is surprising to find that this is very often not the case and that these kinds of insight and their necessary accompaniment, good diagnostic abilities, are often not present. Very often their importance is not emphasized and the theory and techniques that would underpin successful formative assessment are not taught adequately in institutes of teacher education. This fact casts a doubt on how adequate some of our teacher education is. Naturally, a conscientious teacher will, as a matter of course, strive to establish how well pupils have learned what they are supposed to learn. But, if they lack the techniques for doing so effectively through engaging in a penetrating diagnosis of problems or the lack of them, they are unlikely to do as good a job as they might otherwise do.

One final point about formative assessment: it is sometimes thought (White, 1999) that all that the above argument shows is that teachers, if they are serious, need to monitor what pupils learn, rather than assess them. Monitoring could, for example, involve scanning their faces to see if they are interested in or understand what the teacher is teaching them. However, it is not difficult to see that such monitoring would be inadequate to determine whether or not pupils were learning appropriately. One needs some criterion for the truth of the proposition 'pupils have learned what it was intended that they should learn'. Supporting evidence such as 'their faces lit up when they were taught what a quadratic equation was' will not be adequate for such a conclusion. One will need some means of determining whether the learning had actually taken place. Such a method will not be infallible, but it is a minimum requirement that a reasonably safe inference can be made from the assessment to an assertion that the pupils learned what it was intended that they should learn. Monitoring involves observation rather than diagnosis and prescription and cannot do the job of ensuring that a teacher is serious about what they are doing. In this sense, assessment is an intrinsic element of teaching when teaching is taken seriously.

(b) The second primary purpose of assessment is not concerned with the success or otherwise of particular lessons. *It is concerned with establishing whether someone merits the award of a qualification guaranteeing competence and/or knowledge.* This applies both to selection for more education and to admission to an occupation. There are two principal ways of doing this. The first method involves ensuring that candidates fulfil criteria based on the curriculum that they have followed. If they meet those criteria (or enough of them), they are eligible for the award; if not, then they don't. This is usually known as *criterion-referencing.* The second way is to predetermine that a given percentile of the candidates will qualify for the award. The figure could be set at any number, say the top 20 per cent of marks achieved in a test. Then those candidates who find themselves in the top 20 per cent are deemed eligible for the award. The percentage set may be a function of scarce resources available at the next stage of education; it may reflect a judgement on the percentage of the population that can benefit from the next stage, or it may reflect the number of places available in an occupation in a given year. This is usually known as *norm-referencing.*

Criterion-referenced assessment will be looked at in more detail later. It is very important for determining, for example, whether or not someone should be admitted into an occupation. Sometimes, it is combined with norm-referenced assessment, for example when only a percentage of those who meet the criteria are deemed to have reached a high enough standard to enter the next stage of education or to enter an occupation.

Assessment of this kind plays a central role in complex societies like ours, where occupations which we depend on for our safety or our well-being have to be staffed by individuals whom we can trust because of their high level of competence. Professional assessment is a form of 'high-stakes' assessment, because the stakes are high both for society and for the individuals who aspire to enter the occupation.

I take it, however, that Davis has some objections to this use of assessment due to difficulties in establishing whether or not someone really merits the award aimed for or whether or not the assessing authority is justified in withholding the award after a candidate has been through an assessment procedure. The principal difficulties, according to Davis, seem to centre around, first, whether or not an assessment is actually valid – that is that it does actually measure what it purports to measure and second whether or not it is fair. The structure of Davis's argument is that the first question is difficult to answer and because it is difficult, it is also not easy to establish the fairness of assessment. Much of the difficulty identified by Davis hinges on the question of how *valid* assessments actually can be.[1]

It is very difficult for any form of assessment to establish *certainty* of results. By 'certainty' I mean the absence of doubt concerning the conclusions of an assessment procedure. It is important, however, to recognize that *knowledge*, which is what we want from assessment, does not imply *certainty*, otherwise there is little that we could be said to know. It should be noted that in the discussion of formative assessment above, we do not expect competent teachers to arrive at certainty concerning the achievements and difficulties of their pupils. So, what can we expect from a good assessment procedure?

It is reasonable for us to require that it gives knowledge of a student's achievements. This means that we can, for good reasons, believe it to be true and that it is true. 'But', it might be objected, 'we can never establish that it is true, since there is always room for doubt and many 'true' scientific findings are now recognized in fact to be false'. This is, in effect, an appeal to an identification of knowledge

---

[1]We need to negotiate some tricky terminology here. By 'valid' is meant that an assessment procedure actually does succeed in measuring what it purports to measure. In everyday parlance, we would deem a procedure that actually did this 'reliable'. In statistical terminology, 'reliable' only means the 'propensity of a given procedure to give like results in like circumstances'. In everyday parlance, this would of course be another aspect of 'reliability'. I use the more technical terminology to avoid confusion. Where I mean a good quality assessment procedure which is both valid and reliable in the technical sense, I simply call it 'good'.

with certainty alluded to above. The fact that the objection can be formulated so easily, however, testifies to its appeal. How should we respond? I attempt a brief answer.

To say that a proposition is true is *not* to say that it is absolutely true, that is certain for all times and places. Some propositions may indeed have this property (e.g. logically and mathematically true propositions), but it is not a property of true propositions as such. On the other hand, neither should we say that when a proposition is true, it is true only for me or for my immediate community. This position, sometimes known as 'relativism', implies that there is no objective truth of the matter, that is no truth independent of what a person or group takes to be the truth. For this reason, inter-subjective agreement concerning what is true cannot be taken to be a criterion of truth. For a proposition to be true, it must conform to accepted and established procedures for distinguishing between truth and falsity, independently of what anyone at any given time happens to think is true or false. The objectivity of truth rests on a claim that there are certain established ways of determining whether or not propositions are true. It is the use of these procedures (e.g. rules of evidence in a court of law, statistical tests of significance in determining safety margins) that allow us to determine whether a proposition is true or false.

However, it is important to realize that such procedures are not unchangeable, nor are they completely immune from error in their use. In this sense, knowledge is *fallible*, there are circumstances in which a knowledge claim can be defeated, that is shown subsequently to be unjustified. This can arise first when the procedure, despite its being properly used, turns out, on the production of further evidence, to have been faulty in determining truth or falsity. This is simply something that we have to live with for most knowledge claims. It does not absolve us from the responsibility for ensuring that procedures are as good as they can possibly be and that they are used as scrupulously as they can possibly be. It is simply to acknowledge the possibility of post facto error and revision of truth claims which it was perfectly justifiable to make at the time that they were made.

The second type of case is where dissatisfaction arises with the procedure. For example better tests of significance, measuring instruments or experimental procedures have been devised than those previously used. Another type of case arises where the conceptual framework of phenomena under study have been revised, leading to a new way of looking at issues, more or less related to the old way (Kuhn 1962; Rosenberg 2011). Reality is approached through our concern with truth, but our concern with truth and our judgements about what is the best way of establishing truth take different forms at different times (Ellenbogen 2003). In terms of the particular practices that we now have, we can only expect, as Aristotle pointed out (Aristotle, 1925, II, ix, p. 8), the degree of certainty appropriate to the subject matter in hand. In the case of assessment, this is very likely to be something less that complete certainty in our judgements.

How is this relevant to assessment, high stakes or otherwise? Davis might quite justifiably reply that he has never claimed that assessment procedures should yield certainty before they can be applied. Indeed, he has never made that claim. However, if one consistently 'raises the bar' so that no known or widely used assessment procedure is ever good enough to satisfy a critic such as Davis, then we are entitled to think that the extremely high standards demanded are little more than a proxy for a demand for certainty. Davis's claims that test items have little or no validity beyond the test situation, or that transferability of an ability exhibited in a test situation to a wider context fall into this category. It is a form of scepticism which raises persistent doubts about the generalizability of claims made in assessment situations to such an extent that it is difficult to see how assessment could ever be of much practical use. And, one can do this while denying that one denies that transfer from a test situation to an 'everyday' one is possible, simply by claiming (correctly) that one is not making the general claim. But, by making the particular claim that this or that test is not valid over and over again, one is de facto denying the possibility of transfer.

How is this relevant to using assessment to determine whether or not a candidate merits the award of a qualification, which is, in effect, a social guarantee that the candidate knows, can do or understands something? A number of points follow. First, that the procedures for awarding the qualification are as good as they possibly can be consistent with the time and resources available to conduct assessments (and it goes without saying that these must be as generously provided as it is practically possible to provide them). Second, such procedures must be revisable when imperfections in their procedures or results are detected. Third, they can never yield certain results but can yield knowledge in the sense that their outcomes can justifiably be taken to be true.

(c) tracking pupil/student progress towards achievement in a summative assessment (i.e. (b)). Examples would be the use of software packages like ALPS, ALIS, etc.

This form of assessment relies on a version of the kind described in (b) above, that is determining whether or not a student has achieved a particular standard. The difference is that, at the initial stage, the student is not deemed to be eligible for the qualification. The underlying idea with this kind of assessment is that a student's *progress* towards achievement of a qualification is measured. On the face of it, this looks like formative assessment (purpose (a) above), but there are significant differences. Teachers carrying out formative assessment may or may not wish to provide quantitative evidence of achievement, but what they do will depend on how they conduct their teaching. When, however, a measure is used that is intended to give a quantitative judgement about a student's progress, the instrument used is more general and can be used with different classes and different schools. However, the main purpose is still *formative*, and the intention is that strengths and weaknesses in student performance can be identified and weaknesses overcome. Such measures may have other uses, particularly at the level of management of a school or college where decisions about resource allocation may have to be made. Normally, they should not be used as a substitute for day-to-day formative procedures in the classroom.

(d) *Assessing the performance of a teacher, a school, a local authority or a national system.* This can be done, either in terms of end-point achievement or as a measure of progress between two assessment points. It can be done as a synchronic snapshot or as a diachronic exercise. This is one of the major accountability functions of assessment.

With (d) we come to the most controversial aim of assessment and the one that is most in the firing line as far as Davis and other assessment sceptics are concerned. The idea is that measures that attempt to quantify or make precise a student's achievement or progress can also be used to gauge systemic performance of teachers, schools, local authorities or national education systems. There are two issues that we need to keep separate in our minds when forming a judgement about the desirability or workability of such assessments. The first concerns their quality – can they be valid and reliable in the technical senses and can they yield us knowledge? The second concerns the consequences of such assessments, how should they be used? In general terms, the more drastic the consequences of an assessment, the higher the standard of proof required that the results yielded by the assessment instrument do actually constitute knowledge about what the ability or progress of a student should be. In those cases, where the assessment instruments cannot yield the required standard, they should not be used for that purpose.

Measures of progress that take into account student background and prior achievement have rightly been taken to constitute a gold standard of how to judge the performance of educational institutions. Prior achievement is important because statistically it is a powerful predictor of future performance, no doubt because knowledge in most subjects is cumulative and prior acquisitions have a significant bearing on future progress. Student background is important because it serves as a proxy for the social and cultural capital that students and their community bring to the educational situation.[2]

A very important point to make about the kinds of progress measure used is that they are subject to a degree of statistical

---

[2] It is worth noting that this cannot easily be reduced to socio-economic status. Social and cultural capital can vary enormously at the micro neighbourhood level. See Webber and Butler (2007) for more on this.

uncertainty. That means that their results must be interpreted cautiously, so that, for example, one can be 95 per cent confident that progress results for any given school or class fall within a certain range. This means that one can never put an exact figure on either student or school progress, but can only say that, within a (say) 95 per cent confidence interval, results fall within a certain band. Because these intervals are quite broad, it follows that there is a great deal of overlap in performance at both the individual and the school level. As Gray et al. (1996) put it:

> Both the 'effectiveness' and 'improvement' estimates for each school need to be interpreted in light of their inherent uncertainty. Each estimate has an associated standard error.... Only when such estimates are significantly different from zero can one be confident that the school is really different from the population as a whole. At the same time 'bands of uncertainty' (as they are called) can be constructed around the estimates for individual schools. Only when these do not overlap can one be confident that two individual schools are really different from each other. (Gray et al. 1996, p. 47).

The quotation makes it clear that it is not possible to make a meaningful judgement concerning the relative performance of two-thirds of schools in a reference group such as a local authority as there is no significant difference between them on value-added measures. We can conclude that this uncertainty means that they cannot be compared with each other (and therefore be held accountable) on this measure. The point applies with equal force to attempts to measure the performance of individual teachers, local authorities and national systems of education.

Do we conclude from this that 'value-added measures are of no value'? If they do nothing more than replicate the results that can be obtained from raw achievement scores, then this conclusion might be justified. Indeed, some have drawn precisely this conclusion (e.g. Gorard, 2006). However, if we accept that value-added measures that take socio-economic factors into account (contextual value-added or CVA measures) do shed some light on school performance, it does not follow that the difficulty of comparison of the middle range of schools is of no value to those responsible for education.[3] The very fact that one-sixth of schools is significantly underperforming the main group and another sixth is significantly over-performing suggests that CVA could be a useful diagnostic tool for schools themselves, as well as educational planners. Such information can enable schools to begin the process of analysing their shortcomings if they are in the bottom group and all schools can learn from the top performing sixth.

However, all such data needs to be treated with caution. But, this is just as true of measures of achievement which do not take progress into account. As Paterson's (2013) analysis has shown, the type of measure that one uses to assess a school's performance is capable of strongly affecting the relative ranking of that school with others. Thus, a school with an apparently good absolute score at KS4 can look as if it is significantly less well performing under a value-added measure, prompting questions about just how effective it is. The data has value in suggesting lines of enquiry into the causes of school performance. The fact that data needs to be read and interpreted cautiously is not a ground for dismissing it as having no use. Whether it can be used for 'strong accountability' purposes is another matter to which we shall return shortly.

There is some evidence that publicizing school results does have a motivating effect on schools. A study by Burgess et al. (2010) which looked at results in Welsh schools after results ceased to be published suggests that, relative to England, there has been a deterioration in performance, a finding corroborated by the international comparative study PISA, published in December 2013 (Paris, OECD, 2013). On the other hand, the greatest care has to be exercised in the interpretation of statistics on educational achievement. Thus, Chudgar and Quin (2012) examine the comparative achievement of Indian private and state schools. Noting that various studies have found that Indian private schools show a small advantage in educational achievement compared with Government schools, they argue that these studies have not properly compared like with like. Briefly, the technique that they employ in their own study, Propensity Score Matching, takes

---

[3]Gorard's data does not appear to do this, only taking into account prior achievement, which admittedly is a strong predictor of future performance.

account of similarities in composition of classes to be compared. They note that the advantage held by private schools tends to disappear when classes and schools are compared in this way, suggesting that class compositional effects may be an important factor in the apparently superior performance of the private schools.

Making realistic comparisons of like with like in assessing the performance of pupils, schools and teachers is, of course, very important in coming to a realistic and reasonably accurate valuation of educational effectiveness. The point has even more force when a form of accountability which involves punitive sanctions for failure is proposed. For example, in some American states, teachers are annually assessed on value-added achievement scores attained by their pupils. The lowest performing deciles are liable to lose their jobs as the result of such an assessment. Everson et al. (2013) argue that the method through which this is currently managed is flawed as it does not take into account the composition of the classes which teachers actually teach, as opposed to an abstract class which they do not actually teach. They also propose the use of Propensity Score Matching in order to ensure that any individual teacher's performance is based on a comparison with the achievement of classes with similar composition to that which the teacher actually teaches. Only then, do they argue, are educational authorities entitled to make any safe inferences about teacher performance. Even then, they argue, the inferences are not safe enough to justify severe sanctions against underperformance. Instead, such results might lead to a diagnosis of the teacher's performance with a view to improving it rather than punishing the teacher.

It is reasonable to conclude that measuring the individual performances of pupils, teachers, schools and educational systems is an inexact science. That is, it does not and is incapable of providing certainty about the performance of individual entities. We have already noted that knowledge in the sense of *certainty* (being placed beyond any possible doubt) is not an appropriate objective of educational assessment quite generally and still less for the relative assessment of performances, particularly when data is being aggregated (as with classes, schools etc.) and then used to form comparisons. The aggregation of data accentuates the potential for error in any form of assessment and leads to the use of confidence intervals which allow one only to infer that the true result is highly likely to fall within a certain range of possibilities.

This does not mean that what is produced has no worth. It will not be certain and may only give approximate values. This means that for some kinds of situation, such as the application of severe sanctions or the awarding of extravagant rewards, a criterion of *beyond reasonable doubt* is ethically required; it should not be used, even when sophisticated techniques such as CVA or Propensity Score Matching are employed. However, even if such uses of assessment cannot be used for 'high-stakes' purposes, this does not mean that they are of no use. They can be employed for informational diagnostic and improvement purposes with great profit, but the temptation to use them for more than that should always be resisted.

(e) Sorting individuals into different roles in society, educational institutions and employment. This is sometimes done through the same instrument as in (b).

We now turn to the use of assessment (again using the kind of instruments used for purpose (b)) of individual pupil performance for the allocation to individuals of scarce goods. The award of these goods is itself based on an ordinal ranking of individual performances based on individual pupil performance on an assessment. For example the eleven-plus examination leads to individual scores which can then be arranged from lowest to highest. A prior decision, which can be based both on the availability of grammar school places and the presumed desirability of a grammar school place for a given individual, might lead to the allocation of the top two deciles of achievement in the examination to a grammar school place, the remaining 80 per cent to a secondary modern school. Other examples include the allocation of places to sought-after universities, or for prizes or other kinds of reward.

What are we to make of the use of assessment for such purposes? A first observation is that all societies possess scarce but desirable goods for which it is important that there are fair and transparent means of allocation. Whether it is proper to use summative assessments for this does not eliminate the imperative to allocate resources fairly and transparently. A second observation is that a number of factors are likely to contribute to performance, not least being the quality of teaching, the amount of coaching and more generally the deployment of educational resources towards the goal of getting a positive result for all pupils. Differential availability of such goods must cast some doubt on the fairness and transparency of such processes. A third observation is that almost invariably such allocations are made solely on the basis of achievement on a summative assessment, rather than on *progress* whether modified contextually or not. A fourth and final observation is that usually the selection is ostensibly made as a proxy judgement about future potential. Past achievement is taken to be a sufficient sign of future achievement.

These four observations should make us uneasy at the use of assessment for the allocation of desirable goods, however unavoidable it may sometimes seem. In relation to the first observation, the need for fairness and transparency should, at the very least, act as a constraint on the indiscriminate use of assessment for allocating such resources. In relation to the second, we should be worried by the possibility that the ability of some schools and parents to provide large levels of support to pupils entering competitive examinations will give them an advantage which compromises the apparent fairness of the competition. This advantage exists in addition to superior levels of cultural and social capital that such pupils may already possess.

The third observation that there is an argument that progress rather than achievement of a grade at a single assessment point should be one criterion of fairness is one that deserves serious consideration. This point should, however, be made with care, since prior achievement is a powerful predictor of progress and those from already privileged educational backgrounds are likely to have a high prior achievement. Some form of contextualization of progress in terms of levels of cultural and social capital, together with the availability of resources for preparation for the assessment, would ideally be needed in order to bring about the desired fairness.

The fourth point that the usual reason for using such assessments is to assign desirable goods to those who have the greatest *potential* for taking advantage of them is also one that deserves careful consideration. Two conflicting thoughts come into play. On the one hand, prior achievement is a good likely indicator of future performance. On the other, prior achievement may in part be the artefact of the intensive and lavish deployment of educational resources on the pupil. Empirical evidence on this is mixed. A level scores have some predictive ability, accounting for between 9 and 16 per cent of the individual variance in degree classification, and to that extent, are an apparent predictor of potential.[4] But, pupils from comprehensive schools with similar results to those from other kinds of schools also tend to gain higher degree classifications (Sutton Trust, 2010). It is also worth noting that intensive coaching to succeed at A levels is not necessarily a preparation for courses where independent and risky thinking is a desired trait.

Despite the unease which the use of summative assessment for allocation of scarce goods may engender, it is difficult to produce a decisive argument against using it. This is not true of the eleven-plus examination, which was not a good assessment of ability, either in the present, because of the limitations of what it assessed (something like 'general intelligence' or IQ), or of the future, because of the age at which it attempted to make lifelong predictions of ability.

(f) Determining the Suitability of a Candidate to Practise an Occupation.

Although also a form of high-stakes assessment, determining suitability to enter an occupation is also different in a substantial way from the other purposes of assessment discussed in this part of the book. Unlike (e), it is not necessarily related to the allocation of scarce resources, and unlike other forms of assessment, it is not primarily concerned with eligibility to progress to a further level of

---

[4]There is, however, a statistical problem of interpretation in that the data is based on only a very narrow band of A level achievement, since those with no or very low A level results will not go to university.

education. It is also 'high stakes' in the sense that it is often literally a matter of life and death, not only for the aspiring practitioner but also for his clients and for the wide public. It raises issues of its own and will be dealt with separately below.

(b) to (f) could all be classified as 'high-stakes' assessment as the future and well-being of individuals depend on the outcomes.

It is important to distinguish between the *aims* of an assessment practice (i.e. (a) to (f)) and the *instruments* used to fulfil those aims. It is not at all obvious that the same instrument can always be used for multiple aims. We see that many problems arise when either an inappropriate instrument is used for a given aim or when the same instrument is mistakenly used for multiple aims. The latter is clearly a special case of the former.

Transfer and continuing identity of abilities across a range of contexts

One of Davis's main arguments against the use of high-stakes assessments is that the abilities they purport to measure are not manifested, or only weakly manifested outside the context of the assessment procedure (Davis, pp. 10–11). Davis denies that he is a 'transfer-sceptic' who does not believe in the possibility of any transfer of an ability outside a particular context. This may be so in a formal sense, but throughout his writings on assessment, one is aware, as already noted, of a pervasive scepticism concerning the idea that identity of ascribed ability can persist across different contexts. At the most, the contexts in which it does persist are very limited and are problematic when taken from the assessment context to a 'real-life' one. We can take it that *in practice* Davis is some form of transfer-sceptic, ready to challenge any transfer claims on the grounds that context is all important in ensuring identity. He even sets up the continuity of physical objects as an ideal which assessment procedures cannot hope to match for abilities (p. 10), as if the certainty available in this area is a paradigm for education – a paradigm which of course cannot be satisfied. But, this is so because any attempt to do so is like trying to compare apples and pears as a kind of pear.[5] A good example of this scepticism can be found in Davis and Cigman (2008):

> Do we understand the notion of a 'specific ability' which is not *simply* an ability to x or y, but is transferable *from x to y?* What reason do we have to say (or indeed deny) that the ability that now manifests as an ability to y is the *same ability* as that which formerly manifested as an ability to x? (Davis and Cigman, 2008, p. 705).

It is difficult to read this passage as doing anything other than casting grave doubts on the idea that ability-identity can survive from one context to another. The claim is itself ambiguous. Do Davis and Cigman mean that the ability to x and the ability to y are different abilities? If they do, then the claim is empty, since no-one denies that there are different abilities manifested in different contexts. To say, however, that an ability A manifested in context x is the same ability as that manifested in context y is to appeal, as Davis acknowledges, to the criteria of identity that apply to abilities of a certain kind. To say that these are socially and contextually dependent is simply to point to the kind of criteria that they are, it is not to deny that they are valid criteria at all. Davis's claim that he is not a transfer-sceptic is largely empty. This is important as much of his case against high-stakes assessment is very largely based on transfer-scepticism. Indeed, there is an even worse consequence to transfer-scepticism – it is difficult to see how meaningful formative assessment could survive transfer-scepticism either. For example, how would a teacher know that the ability to read which a child manifests in her classroom would be manifested in another classroom with a different text of the same level of difficulty or to reading at home?

Examples of the kinds of abilities where transfer is problematic, according to Davis, include *problem-solving* and *thinking*. However, the problem with these is that it is doubtful whether there *are* any such abilities independent of the kinds of activities in which they

---

[5]Incidentally, this kind of uncertainty of identity is much clearer at the subatomic level in the physical sciences.

are manifested. The fact that these educational chimaeras have been relentlessly pursued by some educators does not mean that they constitute genuine abilities, let alone transferable ones. The ones that we are really interested in for the purposes of gauging the efficacy of what is taught in schools are such abilities as the ability to read, write, count, multiply etc., which are rightly thought to be indicators of success fundamental to taking part in our civilization. Davis presents no evidence that these abilities, as they are learned in schools, are not transferable to other contexts (not necessarily to *every* other context). A few exotic examples, such as the non-transfer of the mathematics of Brazilian child traders, on the one hand and Brazilian school maths, on the other, are by no means sufficient to make such a case. There are deep problems with the ability of British adults to use mathematics and reading/writing abilities in everyday contexts (OECD, 2013), but interestingly enough these difficulties are more pronounced among 18–24 year olds than they are among 55–64 year olds (OECD, 2013, p. 16). A much more plausible explanation for this discrepancy is the ineffective schooling of many 18–24 year olds, rather than a lack of transfer from the school to the everyday and work context. Paradoxically, as we presently see, this may in part be due to the perverse incentives set up by recent performance management targets in England (see Paterson, 2013). There is simply no evidence that there is a widespread problem of transfer of literacy and numeracy abilities beyond the classroom into 'real-life' contexts *as opposed to* failures in schooling. There may be problems with the atrophy of abilities acquired when they are not exercised or perhaps with the lack of familiarity with particular notations in mathematics or particular genres in writing. But, the ability to compute in some notation or the ability to write in some genre are prerequisites of being able to compute or write in others. It is an issue for curriculum designers to work out which range of notations and which range of genres should be handled on the school curriculum, and as is often the case in educational matters, the judgements can be finely balanced.

To summarize this part of the discussion, we need to distinguish between the same task and the same ability. Where tasks are identical (different tokens of what is manifestly the same type), there is little difficulty in transfer, since the same ability is applied repeatedly. An example would be helpful. If someone has to saw the same width of the same kind and thickness of wood in the same circumstances, few would deny that the task and the ability required were identical on different occasions. Where there is variation in task, due to variations in material, requirements and circumstance, then the same abilities may or may not be required; one needs examples to make a judgement about this matter, but what we do know about our abilities suggest that it is perfectly legitimate to suppose that they can be exercised in a wide variety of circumstances and that assessments are able to detect this ability. The ability to drive a car and the driving test (a reasonably 'high-stakes' assessment) is a good example. Davis does not even attempt to maintain that all that a driving test does is to assess the ability of the candidate to perform *these* manoeuvres on *these* streets on *this* day in *these* traffic and weather conditions. Any attempt to deny this would be a *reductio ad absurdum* of his position.

Tasks and abilities do not change significantly over the relevant temporal envelope of an assessment period and they have sufficient stability over a number of years for diachronic comparison to be possible. It should be noted that Davis does not envisage any difficulties with criterion-referenced assessment of musical ability and the continuity and identity of musical tasks. A sceptic could however doubt that musical abilities established in a test could possibly be transferred to a concert setting. But generally, we do not have a difficulty with the idea that such transfer is possible, although we do take account of the different demands of a concert as opposed to a test – we conduct further assessments like auditions to get clearer about this. This points to the fact that sometimes multiple forms of assessment are required for us to become confident about the establishment of an ability. There are cases, for example, where mastery of a *technique* like laying a line of bricks when carried out in the benign conditions of a workshop does not result in the ability to lay bricks in the conditions that are contextually appropriate for a bricklayer, namely under time and cost pressures in adverse weather at heights, etc. We return to this point and its implications for assessment in professional contexts in the section on professional licensure.

We can conclude this section by saying that Davis has failed to make out the case for pervasive transfer-scepticism, either within or beyond educational institutions. Conceptually, his argument rests on an unclarity about what is meant by an ability and the relationship between an ability and the tasks to which it is applied. Empirically, relevant evidence against significant transfer is not forthcoming.

Standards, metastandards and performances

Davis has doubts about whether or not we can make meaningful *comparisons* between performances at different times. When high-stakes assessment is used, for example, to compare the performance of an education system at different times, we rely on a common measuring stick for the two performances. Pring (1992) has expressed doubt as to whether this is possible. What we actually measure, he argues, are *performances* against standards. But, it is incoherent to suppose that we could compare two standards, because there would need to be a standard against which the two standards were measured. This in turn would require a further metastandard to measure the standards and this metastandard would, in turn, require a meta-metastandard against which it could be assessed and so on ad infinitum. But, there is no reason to suppose that one needs a meta-metastandard in order to use a metastandard. Provided the metastandard is sufficiently comprehensive and detailed to capture the characteristics of the standards to be compared, and provided tasks required are sufficiently stable (see points above), then there should be no problem, in principle, about applying the metastandard. So, we can say, for example, that standards have risen or fallen over time according to an agreed metastandard. Performances may seem to have improved, but only if standards by which performances have been measured are held constant (Brown, 2010). It is very important to hold standards constant in any comparison, either synchronic or diachronic. To recapitulate the argument; tasks and associated abilities are identifiable as types across time and different contexts (and we have not seen any good reason to doubt this), they can be used to construct standards (and if necessary, a metastandard) against which performances can be measured. If we wish to compare two standards in respect of the abilities that they are used to measure, then a well-constructed metastandard can be constructed to do just this.

But, Davis raises a further difficulty concerning the high-stakes assessment of schools. It is to be doubted that what we call a 'school' is in fact a stable entity which persists from one year to the next (Davis, p. 41). And, if this is so, then we cannot compare the performances of single schools from one year to the next. We cannot even assess a school's performance on the basis of a rolling three-year average, since each distinct year's performance will relate to a different school. What is one to make of this? Sometimes, it does make sense to talk of a sudden change in a school's identity. 'A completely new school opened on the former site of St. Swithin's school on the 1st September' is an example of a statement that might be made if, for example, there had been a complete change in pupils, catchment area, governors, head teacher and staff from one academic year to the next, even though the building and grounds remained the same.

However, it is misleading to compare school identity criteria with those of physical objects or, indeed, of human beings. The identity is composed of many parts and we do not possess absolute criteria for distinguishing between one school and the next. It makes good sense to say, for example, that 'although the name, the head and the staff all changed over the summer, St. Swithin's is still, in many important respects, the same school, because the pupils and the catchment area remain the same'. In other words, we can talk of schools gradually changing their identity or not changing it much at all over extended periods of time. All that we need is a long enough time envelope to assure ourselves of a school's persistence through time of several years in order to make meaningful comparisons between schools. The lives of local authorities and nation states are, of course, even longer. It is necessary to keep an eye on such matters and ensure that, for example, we don't compare the performance of St. Swithin's ten years ago with that of St. Clement Dane's today, but that is a particular instance of the more general rule that we need to be aware of the fact that schools' identities do tend to change over time and that we must limit our comparisons to relatively short-time sequences. Schools do use intra-school performance comparison software such as ALPS and ALIS to monitor achievement over time. If they were not confident that they were the same school over the time period, then there would be little point in doing so.

Davis expresses great scepticism about whether high-stakes assessment can tell us anything useful. He does so by raising (unjustified) doubts about the identity of tasks, abilities and schools. In a world of flux where nothing is stable, it would indeed be difficult to make any meaningful comparisons. But, this is not how we experience the world, and it is doubtful that what we recognize as experience would exist if such instability were the case. Indeed, it is not just assessment that would be impossible under such conditions. It would not be possible to conduct any empirical research on education which relied on an assumption of the stability of such items. Perhaps Davis is comfortable with this conclusion as are quite a number of people who work in Philosophy of Education. It is a conclusion that is, however, difficult to sustain at either a theoretical or a practical level. It is difficult to sustain at the theoretical level for the reasons just advanced and difficult at the practical level because Philosophers of Education, like other people, wish to make judgements about the efficacy of different schools, particularly if they are considering whether or not to send their children to them.

Knowledge and assessment

We now turn to the central issue of knowledge and its relationship with assessment. It is a truism that one is educated in order to acquire knowledge – but what does this mean? Epistemology has traditionally distinguished three categories: knowledge by acquaintance (KA), knowledge of facts or propositions (knowledge-that or KT) and knowledge how to do something (KH). In fact, professional philosophers' treatments of KA and KH are usually very cursory (Harrison 2013), and the overwhelming focus has been on KT. Philosophical discussion of education generally and of schooling in particular has also tended to focus on KT. Although the emphasis on Davis's work is also in this area, he does bring to bear a welcome distinction between rich and impoverished (or thin) knowledge, which is helpful when we consider questions of the success of any educational enterprise and I make use of that distinction myself.

What does it mean for someone to know a proposition p? The standard answer is that it involves the *truth* of the proposition and a *belief* on the part of the knower that it is true. In addition, a third clause is usually added, that the belief is underpinned in some way, it is justified or has been arrived at via a reliable means (see Everitt and Fisher, 1995, for further discussion). It is sometimes held that one can have justified true belief without knowledge (Gettier, 1963) and various examples have been presented to show how 'epistemic luck' can trump knowledge. We need not trouble ourselves with these debates here but confine ourselves to saying that the ability to justify one's belief is in most cases a necessary condition for knowledge, in addition to belief in the proposition and the proposition's truth. A fundamental point is that knowledge is something more than true belief. True belief is itself something more substantial than ability to recall the proposition; it involves understanding of what the proposition means. Understanding what the proposition means entails that conceptual connections with concepts related to those expressed in the proposition itself are understood, as some of the inferences between the proposition believed and other related propositions. Failure to understand in something more than a minimal sense will undermine anyone's claim to know a given proposition and a fortiori their ability to believe that proposition.

Thus to believe:

Earth is the only habitable planet in the solar system

implies understanding of the concept planet and why the Earth is one. It implies the understanding of the contrast between habitability and non-habitability and of the difference between a star (like the Sun) and planets within its gravitational field (and hence of a gravitational field), and so on.

Inability to appreciate this complexity and interconnectedness is a central flaw in 'learning-outcomes-' based approaches to assessment which rely on recall of individual propositions as a demonstration of knowledge (cf. Coles, 2007). Coles contrasts a learning-outcomes approach which involves recall with a standards-based approach, which provides loose descriptors for potential knowledge of a field for which assessment instruments which aim to sample that knowledge can be constructed. We return to this distinction below.

Davis is on strong ground in insisting on a conception of 'rich knowledge', which is something more than ability to recall a proposition. The ability to recall a proposition verbally or in writing may be sufficient to pass certain kinds of test, but is clearly not sufficient to demonstrate either literal understanding of what the proposition means or the context in which the proposition is embedded and from which it gets its sense. A lack of understanding undermines the claim to believe, since you can't believe what you don't understand. An inability to relate a proposition (which one might *seem* to understand) with the field of knowledge in which it exists also undermines someone's claim to have anything more than minimal understanding of a field.

For example:

A pupil may be able to recall:

Napoleon was crowned Emperor of France in 1804.

But if he does not know who Napoleon was or what an Emperor is, then the claim that the pupil knows the proposition is doubtful. Furthermore, if the pupil is not able to understand that the proposition:

France ceased to be a republic in 1804

follows from the first proposition, or if the pupil is unable to infer, for example, that France styled itself as an Empire from 1804 onwards, then we would have grave doubts about the pupil's claim to knowledge.

Generally speaking, as a broader point about knowledge, we can say that at least part of what we mean when we say that true belief needs to be justified before we can endorse a knowledge claim is that people can make further claims to justify their knowledge. Thus, the pupil can say that because he knows that France called itself an empire after 1804, then it must have had an emperor, and the number of plausible historical candidates for that role was limited to Napoleon. Or, the pupil might emphasize the truth aspect of his knowledge claim and point to the mass of secondary evidence available that Napoleon became Emperor in 1804, and thus infer from the evidence to the truth of the claim.

In the first case, the pupil shows a grasp of internal conceptual connections between, for example, having an emperor and being an empire and of the difference between a monarchy and a republic. In the second case, the pupil demonstrates an understanding of the relationship between historical evidence and a truth claim, and that truth claims can be inferred from evidence. Such seem to be minimal requirements for the claim to knowledge of individual propositions in empirical subjects. To call them examples of 'rich' knowledge is fine if it is used to distinguish the ability to recall from the state of knowing. But, these are actually minimal requirements for a belief to be called knowledge. It should also be noted that these requirements for belief to be called knowledge also strongly imply that the knower has certain practical abilities, most obviously in this case, the ability to infer. So, for example, the pupil should be able to conclude from the fact that France had an Emperor, that it was not a republic, or that given the documentary evidence, it is true that France became an Empire in 1804. The possession of knowledge (let alone subject expertise) therefore requires significant practical abilities on the part of the knower.

The emerging picture of subject knowledge on this view is that it is constituted as a field of interconnected propositions held together, on the one hand, by a network of concepts whose significance is dependent on other concepts, some of which may be more central to the network than others and, on the other hand, by links (themselves conceptually dependent) which provide warrants for the assertion of propositions. It follows that those who learn a subject also acquire the ability to make such links and should be able to deploy that ability as part of their subject knowledge. We now have a picture of what rich knowledge would look like, even for someone who is not a subject expert but who has more than a passing acquaintance with that subject.

What are the implications of this conception of subject knowledge for the way in which we should assess that knowledge, whether it be for high- or low-stakes purposes? As we see, the assessment implications of rich knowledge diverge considerably from what Davis considers them to be. A legitimate target of his objections is the 'learning-outcomes' approach to assessment. In this case, the object of the curriculum is to induce the ability to recall a determinate set of propositions. As we have already noted, this is insufficient even to provide evidence of belief, let alone knowledge since if it is *sufficient* to recall a set of propositions to demonstrate knowledge, then conceptual grasp or the ability to infer from one proposition to another will be unnecessary.

However, since this is not considered to be a respectable way of characterizing subject knowledge and is not widely used in contemporary modern assessment programmes, it is something of an 'Aunt Sally' to consider when critiquing current approaches. Far more common is the use of the Standards approach. The standards approach assumes that subject knowledge is constituted as a field of conceptually interconnected propositions and thus as what Davis describes as rich knowledge. It follows that adequate assessment of such a knowledge field will need to explore whether or not a candidate can indeed understand propositions within the field and make appropriate conceptually based inferences. The question then arises as to what such an assessment approach should be. There are a number of conditions which it will have to fulfil if it is to be adequate. In the first instance, we consider a subject which primarily involves propositional rather than practical knowledge. The latter category raises somewhat different although related considerations. We return to a detailed consideration of these when professional and vocational licensure and qualifications are discussed below.

The first condition is that assessment is concerned with whether or not the candidate *knows* and hence *understands* the propositions within the field. So, at a minimum, it will be necessary to determine that the candidate knows what names and descriptions refer to and what concept expressions mean. The second condition is that the assessment is *comprehensive* and includes knowledge of the whole field of knowledge which is to be assessed. This condition needs to incorporate the requirement that the whole field is to be seen as a unity and that there are connections between all the parts. The third condition is that the assessment is *practically possible*. The fourth and final condition is that the assessment gauges the level of knowledge of the candidate at an appropriate level. In order to do this, we need a statement of the *standard* at which knowledge is supposed to be attained by the candidate. For example, if the candidate is expected to be able to construct a narrative for a particular period (History), or to plan, carry out and report a series of experiments (Physics) or to carry out a certain kind of algebraical calculation (Mathematics), then assessment must ensure that these standards are indeed assessed at the level of difficulty and complexity that they require. Any form of assessment is a compromise between the ideal of completely comprehensive and accurate judgement about a candidate's ability and what is practically possible within constraints of time and expense. So, how do we satisfy these four requirements?

Taking the first condition, we will need to assess understanding either directly or through questioning. However, there is the danger that we will only be assessing recall through this method. An alternative approach will be to make the second condition of *comprehensiveness* the first priority. And, it can quickly be seen that if we assess the range of the candidate's knowledge of the subject, then we will necessarily be assessing *understanding* of individual and groups of propositions as well. We do this by devising assessment instruments that both range across the subject matter and explore the candidate's grasp of connections between concepts, on the one hand, and propositions, on the other. There are a variety of ways in which this can be done, ranging from asking for definitions of key concepts to asking for a more extended demonstration of knowledge such as a report, an essay or a worked calculation. Critical to such assessment will be the monitoring of whether or not the candidate is able to make inferences which show conceptual grasp and an understanding of relations between propositions. In doing so, the understanding of individual concepts and propositions will also be assessed. We can therefore see that the fulfilling the second condition takes account of the first. The third is not so difficult to fulfil, provided we pay close attention to the standards and check and recheck that assessment instruments do indeed satisfy the standard descriptors. Clearly, whether the standards are carefully and clearly described is most important, and those who design the curriculum need to do so with accurate and practical assessment in mind.

The fourth condition however is critical. It will not be possible to assess either the whole curriculum or an individual's most complete grasp of the curriculum material. The best that can be done in almost all circumstances is to sample the candidate's knowledge across the range of the subject. This is another reason why a learning-outcomes approach is inferior. It is impractical to assess the totality of someone's knowledge of a subject in an assessment unless that subject is very restricted in scope. Therefore, a form of sampling, both of the subject matter and of the candidate's knowledge of it is a necessity. In other words, it is necessary to make an *inference* from the candidate's ability to perform the assessment to a conclusion about his knowledge of the subject as a whole, and to do this, it is necessary to construct a testing instrument (e.g. an examination), which samples the range of material in such a way that the candidate can respond authentically, not just employing recall, but demonstrating an ability to make connections across the subject matter. The examination should be based on the standards for what is expected of a candidate working at a certain level within the progression set out in the curriculum, and whether the curriculum is tightly or loosely specified. The English National Curriculum, for example, distinguishes between *programmes of study*, which set out the way in which material is presented in increasing difficulty and complexity and *attainment targets*, which indicate the standards expected at each level.

Thus, in the current English National Curriculum, published in September 2013, there are programmes of study set out in great detail in some subjects such as English and Mathematics. Unlike earlier versions of the English National Curriculum, however, Attainment Targets are less closely specified. This is largely due to disillusionment with trying to specify in detail *levels of achievement* at which it was thought that candidates could be accurately assessed. This relates to assessment purpose (b) described above. The issue here is that there may be sufficient disagreement amongst professionals about which level a pupil has achieved in a particular assessment to make a summative judgement insufficiently accurate. The problem was compounded by an accountability issue. Primary schools were judged by the level at which their pupils achieved in the various subjects and there was an incentive to inflate scores to such an extent that secondary schools did not feel confident in the judgement made. However, there will still be a Key Stage 2 test, so that progress between the end of Key Stage 2 (eleven years of age) and the end of Key Stage 4 (sixteen years of age) can be made.

A properly conducted system of summative assessment will not only sample the material covered in a random fashion, but will also be sufficiently complex in the tasks set to oblige the candidate to show a good grasp of the field as a whole, by making appropriate connections across it. Davis appears to think that there is something inherently flawed in this kind of exercise, even though it is expressly designed to test the 'rich knowledge' of which he (and I) approve (Davis, pp. 28–31). The problem, he claims, is that the candidate will be confronted with questions generated in a random way and this will mean that it is a matter of luck whether he gets assessed in a favourable way. And, since it is a matter of luck, assessments of this kind cannot, by nature, be fair. And, if they are not fair, they are not accurate and, by implication, should not be used for 'high-stakes' purposes.

However, this argument hints at a fundamental misunderstanding of what the point of assessment through the use of an examination is for. We should grant that there are all kinds of cases of poor design and maladministration of examinations, as there are in other walks of life, but this cannot detract from the validity of purpose of an examination that has been properly constructed. Suppose, for example, that a candidate decides on the basis of scrutiny of past examination papers that a certain set of topics will appear on the examination this year. He may be 'lucky' when the questions come up. He may be 'unlucky' when they fail to do so. But, is this an inherent fault in examinations, however well constructed they are? No, it is the fault of the candidate who made an unsuccessful attempt to game the system in which he was operating. He should have made sure that he had grasped the whole range of material to be examined so that he would not be surprised and discomfited by any of the topics that were addressed within the examination.

The implausibility of the contention can be seen in the examination for a driving licence. A would-be driver 'mugs up' parts of the Highway Code that he thinks he will be asked about and finds that he is asked questions about other parts that he has not 'mugged up'. He fails that part of the examination. This is bad luck, but it is his bad luck as a gambler, not the fault of the examination system in sampling from the totality of the code for the purpose of assessing whether someone is competent to drive. If examinations of knowledge of the Highway Code were (or are) game-able, so that candidates can attempt to manipulate the result in their favour and sometimes succeed, then we would have good cause to doubt the probity of the procedure and the consequences for us as a society would be very negative. Davis's critique of examinations from the luck argument is remarkably unpersuasive. It is of course an onerous responsibility on examiners to set examinations that are comprehensive and do not allow patterns to develop over years which give scope for gaming, and it is the responsibility of teachers to cover the whole of the curriculum (more commonly, the syllabus) which is indicated in a programme of study in such way that the candidate emerges with a good grasp. This responsibility is the more onerous in those systems where the curriculum is loosely specified and there is no syllabus, but it is part of a teacher's professional responsibility to ensure that the curriculum is appropriately covered. This, in turn, is part of the responsibility that goes with giving teachers a large measure of professional autonomy in their work, something which I take it that Davis approves of.

Restrictiveness

It might also be argued against the use of examinations that they are inadequate as a means of assessing knowledge in a very broad sense, beyond that captured in the notion of rich knowledge. This will be a very important point when we come to consider assessment for professional licensure below. The thought here is that grasp of a subject matter or of a field is not merely a matter of the grasp of a field of knowledge but involves both *acquaintance* and *know-how*, which if not assessed would fail to capture what is required of someone aspiring to be a subject expert. This requirement I take it is a substantial part of what Lum means by *expansive* assessment of the subject matter (Lum, 2012).

I have a great deal of sympathy with this position. If knowledge of a subject matter does involve acquaintance knowledge and know-how of a certain degree, it is of course desirable that there be means of assessing these, although there may be considerable practical constraints in some circumstances. It is, of course, true that acquaintance knowledge can be assessed through the means of propositional knowledge. Russell (1912) argued that all empirical knowledge by description (propositional knowledge) was ultimately derived from knowledge by acquaintance. Even if we do not accept that this is so in every case, it remains the case that a person's acquaintance with something, if made in a serious and systematic manner, should result in the ability to give a detailed account of the properties of that thing, process, property or whatever, given that we do have the power to describe what we become acquainted with. So, we should not absolutely exclude the possibility that acquaintance may be sometimes be assessed through propositional means.

Likewise, (but we need more care here, for reasons which will become clearer later), we can expect candidates to *describe* a procedure which they know how to carry out as a reasonable substitute for their carrying it out. Describing how to do something should not be identified with knowing how to do it, as some philosophical commentators suggest (e.g. Bengson and Moffett, 2011). Let us say that I know how to F and demonstrate this by doing F. Then (if we exclude flukes, fakes and other odd circumstances) we can say that if A can F, A knows how to F and vice versa. This philosophical view of know-how is, however, thought to be controversial. In particular, it is sometimes argued that if A can describe the procedure for performing F, then A also knows how to F, *even if* A is unable to F. I reject this position. If A can do something, say F, that is a *separate action* from G (A can describe how to F). Being able to F and being able to G, where F and

G are not the same actions, must be counted as separate abilities and, hence, two different forms of know-how. In some respects, the English language is not as helpful with these distinctions as it might be, a point to which we return when discussing professional assessment.

But if this is true, then surely it can't be the case that I can assess someone's knowledge of how to do something by assessing their ability to give an account of how to do that thing? However, matters are not that simple. When I say that someone knows how to do something, I radically underdetermine the detail of what doing that thing actually involves. As pointed out earlier, types of actions and types of ability that underlie the performance of those actions are variable according to the individual performing them and also according to the circumstances of performance. Our criteria for the identity of activities and abilities are different from those for the identity of physical objects, but this does not make them any less useable. It follows therefore that we cannot directly assess the infinite variety of ways in which abilities are exercised, token by token. We have to infer from an individual performance what the likelihood is that the candidate will continue to perform in an appropriate (or excellent) way in future and varying circumstances. So, ability to F in one case will be a sound basis for inferring that the ability can be exercised in others (we exclude the possibility that performance in one instance is a fluke, a fake, a fraud or subject to some other anomaly such as freak weather conditions or whatever).

However, there will also be circumstances in which we would think that it is unsafe to infer the ability in another context from performance in one. Cases where this is important include those where the field of activity is particularly varied, complex and unpredictable and requires the application of specialist knowledge to particular circumstances. In such cases, we often need to rely on what the candidate *would* do *were* he to be put in those circumstances. Examples include choosing the right kind of instrument for a particular token of the task type, or judging the appropriate dosage for a patient or the stopping distance of a vehicle in particular hypothetical circumstances. However, we do not normally infer from the hypothesized response *alone* to the ability. We take the fact that the candidate is able to perform in certain circumstances which have been observed *together with* his account of how he would respond in hypothetical circumstances as jointly giving us good grounds for holding that he is able to perform in those hypothetical circumstances.

So, we can see that it is permissible to use a candidate's knowledge-that as evidence for know-how or acquaintance knowledge in certain circumstances. We do, of course, need to be careful about the degree of inferential warrant that the evidence permits and this is of high importance in professional contexts. But, for the moment, it is worth establishing the principle that knowledge-that can serve as a substitute for other epistemic abilities in certain circumstances. Examinations are one instrument among others for carrying out this kind of assessment, and although they seem to be restrictive with respect to the kinds of knowledge and ability that they are capable of assessing, this restrictiveness need not mean that they are not useful forms of assessment, albeit indirect, provided that they are used with care and, in many cases, combined with other forms of assessment.

No-one is claiming that it is easy to construct effective examinations. The discussion above should give the reader a pretty good idea of where the challenges lie. However, the arguments against their use, ranging from the rich knowledge requirement, to the claim that they give too great a role to luck, to the claim that they are excessively restrictive in relation to the kind of knowledge that they purport to assess, have all been shown to be without foundation.

Assessment for professional purposes

We want to know whether someone is competent to practise a certain occupation. It is often thought necessary, because of the importance of the occupation, to provide a public guarantee that an individual does in fact possess the knowledge and ability to practise the occupation in a manner that is both safe and guarantees that the goods provided by the occupation have reached a sufficient standard of quality. Naturally, we expect such a guarantee for occupations which have a major impact on health and public safety such as Medicine and Aircraft Piloting, but we may also find them in other cases, although the range of such cases varies from country to country. Thus, it is common in countries such as Germany and the Netherlands to require a qualification which acts as a licence to practise in such activities as bricklaying or hairdressing. And, of course, we all recognize the need for a licence to practise driving any kind of vehicle on the road and a special licence for the drivers of heavy goods vehicles. Train drivers too have to be assessed and tested on their knowledge of particular routes, even when they have achieved the qualification necessary to become a driver.

In all these cases, the qualification acts as a social guarantee that the individual is competent in those activities that the qualifications state the holder to be competent in. It is difficult to see how modern life could be conducted without such practices. The only sure way in which one can guarantee that someone is indeed competent is through a form of assessment. Such an assessment is indeed 'high stakes', both for the individual who wishes to practise an occupation and for society which depends for its well-being and sometimes safety on the competence of the practitioner. Because of these high stakes, it is important that the assessment is rigorous so that there is a very high degree of probability that the candidate who is successfully assessed can indeed practise competently. Some of the challenges to doing this have been mentioned in the section above. They include:

The complexity and variety of the activities (and the situations in which those activities are required) particular to the occupation.

The fact that knowledge as well as know-how is required and this knowledge needs to be manifested in successful professional action.

To these requirements may be added the fact that the occupation may well change over time and the need for practitioners of the occupation to co-ordinate their activities with those of other, cognate occupations (e.g. doctors and nurses, bricklayers and carpenters, drivers and mechanics).

There is a huge variety of practices amongst different countries concerning which occupations need a rigorous licence to practise obtained through a qualification. Some countries include a huge range of occupations in such a requirement while some, like Britain, tend to focus on some of the professions and some safety-critical occupations like gas-fitting. All developed countries are, however, agreed that qualifications underpinned by rigorous assessment are indeed required in some occupations. The questions arises therefore as to what extent such assessments can be relied upon. It is worth noting that such assessments do not necessarily regulate entry into an area where there is a scarcity of positions (although this may be the case), unlike assessment of type (e) above. Such assessments do, however, require a comprehensive and accurate account of the candidate's knowledge and ability (like type (b) above). Unlike either of these, however, such assessments must be capable of guaranteeing performance in a variety of conditions, not just in academic situations. The question of *transfer* therefore becomes critical in appraising the possibility of successful assessment.

We have already noted Davis's scepticism (if not outright denial) of the possibility of significant degrees of transfer. Significant transfer is important for all the reasons mentioned above. The complexity and variety of the situations in which know-how is exercised necessarily means that there is a great deal of variation in the ways in which the relevant know-how is exercised. Furthermore, it is often the case that an individual needs to be able to judge whether or not to perform a certain activity, depending on the circumstances. Judgement and discretion concerning whether, when and what to do are a central part of professional activity in many cases. However, the complexity is greater than that in the many cases where knowledge is required for professional practice.

The judgements that one makes and the subsequent actions that one takes depend on how successful one is in bringing to bear relevant knowledge onto the requirements of particular situations. A doctor has to use medical knowledge as well as acquaintance with the immediate evidence to diagnose a condition. An army officer has to use knowledge of logistics, enemy capabilities and topography to judge the likely dispositions of an opposing force and to make his own dispositions accordingly. A mason (in France) will need to use his knowledge of materials, geometry and mechanics in order to successfully construct a two-storey building.[6] Those assessing professional competence face the challenge, not only of assessing the possession of relevant professional knowledge, but also of the ability of the candidate to successfully deploy that knowledge in practice. We should not forget the importance of qualities of character in exercising judgement and discretion. In assessing an individual's competence, we are making a judgement about their dispositions to act in a range of circumstances, dependent on how we evaluate certain features of their character such as *adaptability, determination, cooperativeness, conscientiousness, discretion* to name but a few. The degree of transfer involved here is high, and if we are justified in scepticism about transfer, then the possibility of successful assessment of professional competence is compromised. But, there is a third issue that assessment of professional competence has to take account of. Most occupations undergo evolution according to social, economic and technological change. Workers in the construction industry need to understand new building techniques, for example those associated with low-energy usage, changes in ways of working and, if they are migrant workers, new languages and cultures. How can it be possible to assess such qualities, which seem to some extent to involve *thinking skills* about which Davis, with some justification, has already expressed scepticism? There are, then, a number of issues that need to be addressed in showing how good assessment for competence to undertake professional practice is possible by giving a proper account of transfer.

Assessing complex practices

How does one begin to go about thinking about assessment when it involves activities of such complexity as those involved in professional

---

[6]'Aim of the vocational education (for the bricklayer/mason in France – CW) To develop professionals qualified in bricklaying capable of building a structure or part of a structure two storeys high, including bricklaying and masonry, reinforced concrete structures, necessary fittings, cladding, piping and ventilation shafts ... .' This is an official description of the aims of the CAP Maçon, available, for example on: http://www.cfbtp-lemans.com/product/certificat-aptitude-professionnelle-maconnerie/

practice? A useful starting point is the observation that occupations are examples of *normative activities* (Baker and Hacker, 1985), or what are sometimes called rule-governed activities. Characteristic of them is that there are correct and incorrect ways of carrying them out and that correct ways are also subject to norms of appraisal in terms of a perceived standard of excellence. How is one inducted into a normative practice in such a way that one understands how one is to act independently within it? The brief answer is that, although training in the right responses is part of the story, as one becomes more proficient and able to make independent judgements, it is still possible to reference one's individual performance against the wider practice, so that one's activities are recognized as part of the occupational practice by other practitioners. One cannot make arbitrary decisions concerning what is the appropriate way to go on without regard to the expectations of authoritative members of the practice (Kripke, 1982).

Among other things, this means that one learns to recognize professional situations as being of a type (e.g. this patient is presenting with symptoms of X) initially by subjecting one's own judgement to the validation of experienced practitioners and later, when one has attained a degree of independence in practice, by benchmarking one's own performance against the norms set by generations of experienced practitioners. One's own interpretations of particular situations come to be shaped and validated by the interpretations of experienced practitioners. Thus, one does indeed develop the ability to think about practice in a variety of situations. But, this means that one develops relevant abilities to *interpret, select, assess* and *justify* decisions made as part of professional practice. The thinking that one does must be transferable from one type of professional situation to another. This does not imply that one is exercising some kind of generic thinking skill, however. This will only seem problematic if one insists on aligning the criteria of identity of professional situations with those of physical objects, in which case, of course, one must fail the test of both token and type identity.[7] A person fails the test

---

[7]'Token identity' meaning that they are literally 'the same thing' as in 'the same cat as I saw in the garden yesterday', 'type identity' meaning, for example, it was the same creature (i.e. a cat) as I saw in the garden yesterday (i.e. a member of the same species, not necessarily the same individual cat).

of token identity because there is no necessary spatio-temporal continuity between one situation and another, and that person may well fail the type identity test because situations will have overlapping similarities and differences that may well resist the easy specification of necessary and sufficient conditions for situation A and B being of the same type. Nevertheless, the occupational practice may well determine what counts as being the same type of situation.

In the typical professional situation, one's occupational knowledge will be brought to bear on one's decisions and actions. But, the relevant knowledge will very likely have originally been acquired in a classroom rather than in practice. How then can it be transferable from classroom to practice while remaining the same knowledge? The situation is surely much more complex than the requirement for a candidate to cite at a later date what he has learned at an earlier one. The answer to this apparent conundrum is contained in what has just been argued for in relation to making judgements about situations. One learns to apply knowledge acquired through the experience of being in situations in which judgements about what one is faced with and what one needs to do are encountered and negotiated. Initially, this will probably require a great deal of guidance and advice, which will, it is hoped, be less needed as experience is gained. In due course, the apprentice will come to make more independent judgements and may be required, with decreasing frequency, to provide a post hoc explanation of why a particular course of action was chosen. In due course, the candidate will be a fully fledged professional, able to make and self-justify such decisions.

This line of reasoning might prompt the thought that assessment of professional competence should only occur at the point at which the candidate is, to all intents and purposes, fully launched on their professional career and that the 'high-stakes' assessment need be nothing more than an official 'sign-off' by an experienced mentor, that all is well with the candidate's professional practice. This line of thinking might be reinforced by a claim of Gilbert Ryle's:

A man knowing little or nothing of medical science could not be a good surgeon, but excellence in surgery is not the same thing as knowledge of medical science; nor is it a simple product of it.

The surgeon must indeed have learned from instruction, or by his
own induction and observations, a great number of truths; but he
must also have learned by practice a great number of aptitudes.
(Ryle, 1949, p. 49)

If we were to think along these lines, then assessment of the 'great
number of aptitudes' in practice conditions that such a surgeon
had acquired in practice conditions would be sufficient to ensure
that competent surgeons were able to enter independent, full-time
practice without any further supervision. The interesting question,
though, is why this is not how we certify surgeons, or, indeed, most
other professions. In order to get clearer about this, it will be helpful
to scrutinize Ryle's claim more closely.

(1) 'excellence in surgery is not the same as knowledge of medical
science; nor is it a simple product of it'

Few would dispute this claim. Indeed, the usual story about
professional expertise is precisely that a professional is able to put
his relevant subject knowledge (e.g. medical science) to work in his
professional practice.

The next relevant part of the quotation is:

(2) 'The surgeon must indeed have learned from instruction, or by
his own induction and observations, a great number of truths ... '

The crucial phrase here is 'by his own induction'. If the aspiring surgeon
could indeed acquire medical science through induction based on
medical experience, then one could make out a case for claiming that
theoretical instruction in the classroom was not necessary. So long
as a sufficient amount of experience was provided for opportunities
for induction to take place, and the candidate had the ability to make
these inductions, then theoretical instruction would not be needed.
But could this in fact be the case?

It is worth reflecting on the difference between induction and
deduction in order to be clearer about this. Greatly simplifying,
suppose that the 'truths' on which an occupation or profession rest

can be set out in a thousand propositions: $P_1 ... P_{1,000}$.[8] Given sufficient time we could ensure that the candidate knew these propositions and we could also give him the wherewithal to acquire new ones as they became available. Armed with this knowledge, the candidate should be able to recognize professional situations where one or more of these truths was relevant to practice. Even in cases where an unexpected, especially complex or unique situation were to arise, the candidate would be able to fall back on his knowledge in order to determine a course of action, provided that the truths in which he had been instructed were sufficiently comprehensive. Of course, we must add the rider that the candidate must also be able to apply these truths to practice. But, on this model, novice practice is precisely about acquiring this ability. However, he would, in due course be able to reason along the following lines:

1   This is a situation of type S

2   P_3 is relevant to S situations

3   In all S situations, P_3 indicates that course of action A is most appropriate

4   Therefore, do A

It is worth reflecting on this. We assume that the candidate does indeed acquire the 'truths' relevant to practice. However, we would also expect the theoretical element of the programme to include propositions like (2). In other words, candidates can also be instructed in the relevance of truths to professional situations. This does not of course mean that they can, all by themselves, judge what the type of professional situation is. Instruction may help, but controlled professional experience is also most likely to be necessary. A similar point is true of (3). Instruction may help with this, but controlled professional experience is also likely to be important. Armed with truths and practical experience, the candidate is able to make deductive inferences in the course of professional practice.

---

[8]This is simplified both in reducing professional knowledge to such a small number of propositions and also in ignoring the inferential connections between them (see the discussion above).

The candidate learns relevant truths beforehand. These, when combined with relevant professional practice, lead to deductive style professional judgements.

Induction involves generalizing from singular cases to universal or near-universal statements or, alternatively, accumulating truths through acquaintance with singular instances. How would this work? First, candidates would have to be confronted with a range of widely differing professional situations. Second, they would have to devise a course of action based on acquaintance with situation S. Having done so on numerous occasions accompanied by a successful intervention, they could go on to conclude that a proposition, say P_3, was relevant to their success and go on to generalize along the lines of (3) above, that in all S type situations, P_3 indicates that A is the appropriate course of action. If this was a plausible method of professional education, then assessment of practice in a sufficiently wide range of situations would be sufficient to license someone to practise. But, we generally do not do this – why?

This is not difficult to see. First, the candidate would need to be exposed to the full range of professional situations that could be encountered. This is unlikely to be the case in any complex occupation. Second, assuming that it did happen, the candidate would have to conclude that P_3 was relevant and that P_3 indicated that S was the appropriate course of action. It is hard to see how, on the basis of experience alone, and without the benefit of any professional knowledge, that the candidate could either derive relevant propositions which would be of a general nature on the basis of limited experience or be able to work out how they were relevant to professional action. Furthermore, there is the danger that the derivation of relevant truths would be done in isolation leading to acquaintance with propositions that, even if they were true generalizations (which would be problematic given their derivation in a limited number of situations), would not be sufficient to give the candidate the wide range of inferential understanding (what Davis has called 'rich knowledge') necessary for useful employment of interconnected bodies of subject knowledge. It is not difficult to see how such a form of professional education, except for the most simple and restricted of occupations, would be extremely lengthy, error-prone and inefficient. This is why we do not educate surgeons so that they learn relevant truths and courses of actions associated with them through their own inductions and observations.

What do these considerations imply for the assessment of occupational and professional qualifications? An initial observation is that they are inevitably 'high stakes'. First of all, for the individual concerned, since the achievement of the qualifications, especially if it is also a 'licence to practise' is a condition for obtaining a livelihood in that occupation. Second, for society, since providing the qualification is tantamount to the provision of a guarantee that the individual can practise the occupation safely and efficiently. This is particularly the case where safety is important, or where valuable and highly expensive equipment is placed in the hands of practitioners. Those areas where a background of useable systematic knowledge is deemed to underpin practical activity as is the case, for example, in the German dual system of apprenticeship means that, at the very least, there has to be an assessment of how the candidate is able to put the relevant systematic knowledge into practice.

In assessing professional qualifications, two kinds of risk resulting from assessment error need to be considered. The first is that the candidate will wrongly be deemed not to have successfully completed the requirements needed for the qualification. The second is that an unsuitable candidate is deemed to have merited the qualification, thus securing a guarantee of fitness to practise. While the first risk is obviously one that the candidate is most anxious to avoid, the risk to the society of there being significant numbers of incompetent practitioners around, particularly in areas where the well-being of the public and clients is at stake is of greater consequence. Therefore, the balance of error avoidance has to be on the side of the public, ensuring that the assessment process is sufficiently rigorous to reduce the risk to the public as much as possible.

These considerations suggest the following:

Given that the candidate has to have a secure grasp of theory as 'rich knowledge', and given that we cannot securely assess this just in terms of in situ performance, candidates will have to be examined on this knowledge much in the way in which it is done for other assessment purposes. Such knowledge should also include knowledge of how to apply the relevant systematic knowledge to problems of professional practice, even if they have not actually been encountered in practice. Second, the candidate also needs to demonstrate their ability to apply their theoretical knowledge to practise in a variety of complex and unpredictable situations in realistic conditions. Ability to do this will have to inform the inference to a conclusion of general professional competence, together with abilities demonstrated in the first element of assessment. The 'inferential gap' that opens up, between what is known about a candidate's performance in realistic conditions in a limited range of situations and the candidate's hypothetical response in a wide variety of presumed situations has to be as narrow as possible. In particular, we need to be sure that the candidate can operate in realistic conditions and, crucially, possesses the ability to apply theoretical knowledge to decisions about professional courses of action in such conditions.

There is an important point about know-how we have already remarked on. 'To know how to do something' is ambiguous in English between two senses. The first is that 'know how to F' is to be able to do F. The second is that of 'being able to give an account of how to F' which is another ability. Assessment of professional practice needs to establish that ability is exercised over a wide range of requirements in a wide range of situations. Inference to this ability has to be secured through showing that the candidate knows how to (is able to) perform successfully for a wider variety of actions. As they cannot all be directly assessed, it is the evidence of 'know-how' in this first sense, with 'know-how' in the second sense ranging over a wide variety of possible requirements that justifies the assessor in saying that A knows how to practise the occupation.

The first condition for professional knowledge suggests that, in order for an assessment to be sufficiently comprehensive, it needs to be conducted through an instrument such as an examination. The examination will need to ensure that the range of relevant knowledge is adequately sampled. The issue of whether the candidate experiences 'bad luck' in failing to secure questions that he can answer adequately can be dismissed. The candidate has to demonstrate a full grasp of the knowledge relevant to the practice of the occupation, and if he has not bothered to acquire this, then he should not, in any event, be awarded the qualification. Thus, for example, it is perfectly reasonable to examine the candidates on the ways in which they would approach such-and-such a hypothetical situation which would typically (or even uncommonly) occur in professional practice.

The second condition should by now be self-evident, that the candidates be able to show that they are able to meet a range of professional requirements in realistic conditions, such as they might reasonably expect to encounter in professional practice for example through evaluation of professional conduct in situ in operational conditions.

Conclusion

We are now in a position to draw some conclusions from this discussion.

- *We should distinguish between different aims of assessment and instruments for attaining those aims.*

'Assessment' is a term that covers a fairly broad family of practices which have different, although sometimes related, purposes. An instrument should be literally 'fit for purpose', and therefore we cannot assume that an instrument fit for one purpose will be fit for another. One of the problems with the use of assessment is that very often the wrong instruments are used for the particular purpose at hand, when, for example a high-stakes instrument is used for informal formative assessment or vice versa.

- *Formative assessment is a necessary part of teaching.*

This was established through a detailed argument and it was also shown that monitoring could not be a substitute for assessment. It follows then that all serious preparation for teaching should involve giving teachers the ability to assess the progress of their pupils with a view to diagnosing their strengths and weaknesses with a view to addressing them effectively. This implies that they should be able to devise and use techniques appropriate to the children that they happen to teach. Instruments used for this purpose should not normally be used for other forms of assessment.

- *Assessment can never attain certainty (Dearden's 'inferential hazard' - Dearden, 1984). We need to beware of a destructive scepticism about attaining knowledge of educational matters.*

It is futile to expect certainty from assessment procedures. As with all methods of testing fallibility is to be expected. This usually involves a balance of risk – on the one hand the risk of denying someone an opportunity or good to which they are entitled by their performance and on the other denying others (or society) a good to which they have a right. How the risks are managed should depend on the balance of harm. If the risk to others and society is small, then the assessment should minimize the risk of a 'false negative' judgement on the candidate for assessment. If the risk to society is great for a 'false positive' judgement that a candidate has achieved a standard when in fact he has not, then the risk to society should be minimized.

- *There is not just one form of 'high-stakes' assessment. The issues are different for: assessment of teachers, assessment of schools and assessment for professional competence.*

We can distinguish four forms of 'high-stakes' assessment. First, Establishing whether someone merits the award of a qualification.

Where the risk to society is small, but the consequences to the individual are momentous, the risk of a 'false negative' should be minimized. Systems should not place unnecessary barriers in the way of certification of individual achievement *provided no-one else's interests are affected*. In practice, though, this might be difficult in the case of competition for scarce goods. Here, all candidates' interests have to be treated the same and since minimizing the false negatives could mean increasing them for others, in practice a system that disadvantages any given candidate as little as possible is to be preferred. Society as a whole's risk is relatively low, so the barrier to achieving the qualification should not be too high. However, access to the desirable goods unlocked by the qualification may have to be determined by relative performance (see below). But, this consideration only makes the need to treat all candidates as impartially as possible the more pressing.[9]

- *Determining the Suitability of a Candidate to Practise an Occupation.*

In this case, the risks to society can be considerable if an incompetent person is allowed to practise for a lifetime, particularly in a safety critical context. In this case, the dangers of a 'false positive' result should be minimized and the success criterion should be high, even at some risk to the candidate.

- *Assessing the performance of a teacher, a school, a local authority or a national system.*

The instrument to do this is usually some form of achievement measure which allows for the construct of a progress measure. Much has been written about the large margins of uncertainty that are endemic to these forms of assessment and the methodological difficulties of ensuring a fair means of determining performance, not to mention the possibilities of 'gaming' results. The risks of error are high and the interests of teachers and schools particularly can be seriously threatened by the use of faulty techniques to determine performance. Such 'high-stakes' measures should therefore be used very sparingly and where they are used should ensure that false negative results are minimized.

- *Sorting individuals into different roles in society, educational institutions and employment.*

In situations like this, the individual's interests are most at risk. However, failure to secure the relevant desirable goods is bound to be the lot of many of the candidates. In this case, as in the case of assessment to merit the award of a non-professional or non-vocational qualification, the emphasis should be on ensuring that the assessment procedure does not favour one type of candidate more than another.

---

[9]What actually counts as impartiality may be problematic. Should there be compensatory procedures for certain kinds of disadvantaged candidates, for example?

- *We need to give the underlying purposes of assessment more attention than they currently receive.*

This point should be obvious from what has been said before. Assessment is a family of related practices, organized around distinct, but often related purposes. The means used to realize those purposes should be as appropriate as possible to the purposes, and there should be no parsimony involved in using a limited stock of instruments if there is any doubt concerning their overall fitness for purpose.

Afterword: Can the Two Positions be Reconciled?

Gerard Lum

Andrew Davis's ongoing critique of high-stakes assessment will find much support amongst those who instinctively believe that such assessment, to the extent that serves its intended purpose of allowing comparisons to be made between schools, threatens to distort the processes of teaching and learning to the detriment of children's education. Likewise, Christopher Winch's carefully considered defence of the various uses of assessment will be welcomed by those who share his view that assessment, including assessment for accountability purposes, is vitally important for education and for society at large. Yet, I suspect that there may also be some who while concurring entirely with Winch vis-à-vis the possibility of meaningful assessment and its critical role in education, nevertheless share with Davis the intuition that there is something profoundly and irredeemably problematic about using assessment for accountability purposes. In what follows, I explore whether by characterizing the problem of assessment for accountability somewhat differently it might be possible to reconcile these seemingly incompatible positions and resolve this apparent impasse. I try to show why I think Davis is essentially correct in his intuition that there is something fundamentally wrong-headed about the use of assessment for accountability purposes, whilst at the same time agreeing entirely with Winch about the possibility of meaningful assessment and its indispensable place in education. Although demonstrating that Davis's instincts in this matter are essentially correct, I take issue with the way in which he frames his argument. Accordingly, much of the ensuing discussion focuses on matters arising from Davis's contribution by way of considering how we might revise the argument against the use of assessment for accountability purposes in schools.

As we shall see, this revision involves challenging some long-established ways of thinking about assessment and assessment methodology. In order to understand what it is exactly that is wrong with such uses of assessment, it is suggested that we need to question our current understanding not only of the *kinds* of assessment at issue, but of what we actually *do* when we engage in the practice of assessment, and even more fundamentally, what we mean when we speak of assessing 'knowledge'. Getting clear about this, I suggest, has far-reaching implications not just for the processes we use to hold schools to account but for our use of assessment more generally, including the way in which we assess vocational and professional capability.

It is worth mentioning at the outset that one important difference between Davis's position and the position to be developed here is that whilst Davis's argument has generally been regarded as a critique of high-stakes assessment per se, in contrast I argue that there are very specific reasons for questioning the plausibility of assessment for accountability purposes in schools, reasons that have little or no bearing on the use of high-stakes assessment more generally. The claim that any sufficiently valid process of assessment will inevitably lack the level of reliability required for high-stakes purposes, a claim that has featured in many of Davis's writings on this topic, was rebuffed by Randall Curren (2006) precisely on grounds that there are a good many high-stakes situations where we would not contemplate abandoning the procedures even though we recognize that those procedures could never be completely reliable. As Curren says, the determining of a defendant's guilt or innocence in a court of law, or the assessment of medical students' fitness to practice certainly have high stakes, both for society and for the individuals concerned. Such procedures are not entirely reliable but it precisely because the stakes are high that we are prepared to accept arrangements that are deemed to be reliable *enough*. As we shall see, when the problem with high-stakes assessment in schools is more clearly identified, Curren's examples actually illustrate the case *against* the use of assessment for accountability purposes. But for the moment, the main point here is that whilst Davis's position – particularly in its earlier incarnations – might be seen to militate against the use of assessment for high-stakes purposes per se, I try to show that the problem that is fundamentally at issue arises when assessment is used to hold schools and teachers to account.

In this book, Davis begins his critique of high-stakes assessment by querying a supposed relationship between test scores and 'real improvements in adult knowledge' (p. 12). If the purpose of education is to provide the kind of knowledge adults need in order to play a useful role in a competitive industrial economy – and here Davis is surely playing devil's advocate because he would certainly acknowledge that education has a good many other important aims – then we can take it that governments promoting such aims should believe that 'better test scores' mean 'real improvements in adult knowledge' (p. 12). He goes on to argue that there are reasons to doubt the feasibility of this relationship because in order to transfer knowledge from one context to another, from the classroom to the workplace, that knowledge needs to be characterized by a certain 'connectedness'. On Davis's view, this is the characterizing feature of 'real', 'rich' or 'genuine' knowledge', in contrast to the kind of knowledge that would merely allow a pupil to proffer a correct answer to a test question. The latter, according to Davis, should properly be thought of as 'thin' knowledge. The danger, on Davis's view, is that schools under pressure to improve their standing in school league tables will be inclined to shift from teaching 'real knowledge' to inculcating in their pupils a 'limited range of performances' or 'set of procedures' (p. 34) so as to obtain better results in tests.

Now, there are several things we might question about this. First, it is not at all clear that the rationale for testing is grounded in an assumed relationship between what is tested and the knowledge adults are supposed to need in the way that Davis suggests. It might be said that inasmuch as tests are related to anything, they are related to attainment targets delineated by the National Curriculum. The National Curriculum specifies what is thought to be worth teaching, and tests are configured in such a way as to determine whether pupils have or have not learnt what they are meant to have learnt. Now, it may be that there are grounds to question whether or to what extent the National Curriculum corresponds with what we perceive to be the proper ends of education – whether those ends are related to employment, culture, citizenship or anything else. But, in and of itself, this is not an assessment problem: this is the rather different matter of whether the attainment targets of the National Curriculum correspond sufficiently with what we take the ends of education to be.

The second thing here relates to the *kind* of assessment ostensibly at issue. As Davis acknowledges, the processes at issue are criterion-referenced in that their purpose is to determine whether or not the learner has achieved what they are meant to have achieved. Davis's complaint is that 'we are generally unable to make exact and detailed predictions about the degree of transfer between school performances such as test responses, and successful activity in everyday adult life' (p. 31). The difficulty with this, however, is that it is not the purpose of criterion-referenced assessment either to make such predictions or to be evaluated in these terms. Criterion-referenced assessment is intended merely to determine whether the learner does or does not know the thing that has been identified as worth teaching. Accordingly, many will fail to see any difficulty here: if we acknowledge that we want the learner to know *x* or to be able to do *y*, then what can be inappropriate about using assessment to determine whether they *do* know *x* or *can* do *y*?

It is clear that underpinning Davis's argument is the intuition that high-stakes assessment somehow causes a distortion of the education process such that that which gets taught is in some sense qualitatively different from or at some remove from what we would ideally want learners to know. Articulated in the first instance as a discrepancy between the kind of knowledge amenable to being demonstrated by pupils in the classroom and the kind of knowledge that adults in a competitive industrial economy actually need, the discrepancy is further delineated, first, in terms of the important sense in which all knowledge is essentially context-dependent – classroom knowledge thus being very different from workplace knowledge – and second, in terms of the distinction Davis draws between 'rich' and 'thin' knowledge. And, it is by way of delineating this latter distinction that he invokes the idea of the 'connectedness' of knowledge, such connectedness being a characterizing feature of 'rich' as opposed to 'thin' knowledge.

The idea that knowledge consists of interconnected propositions could almost be regarded as a central plank of Anglo-American analytic philosophy and philosophy of education. This conception of knowledge has not only been a mainstay of Davis's ongoing critique of high-stakes assessment but it is similarly invoked by some of Davis's staunchest critics. Christopher Winch for example, in this volume, similarly refers to the 'interconnectedness' (p. 83) of knowledge. Yet, I want to suggest that resort to this 'interconnected knowledge thesis', as we might call it, ultimately serves to misrepresent what it is that is problematic about the use of assessment for accountability purposes. If we are to get clearer about the nature of this problem, we need to look more closely at this conception of knowledge.

What is 'interconnected' knowledge?

One of the things that is puzzling about this conception of knowledge is that it is not at all clear what it is for someone to 'know that p' – where 'p' is a proposition such as 'It is raining' or 'The Battle of Hastings was in 1066'. By way of illustration, let us imagine four very different instances of individuals able to provide the correct answer to the question 'When was the Battle of Hastings?'

(i)   *Polly is a parrot who knows that if she says '1066' whenever her mistress makes a certain kind of utterance she will be rewarded with a peanut. Polly enjoys being made a fuss of and she also likes peanuts…*

(ii) *Jack is a five-year-old pupil who is eager to proffer the answer '1066' to his teacher. He doesn't know what or where 'Hastings' is; neither does he know what '1066' means – he has heard grown-ups talk about 9/11, perhaps 1066 is like that. He certainly knows what a 'battle' is: guns and tanks, and ray guns; he saw Cybermen on television…*

(iii) *Peter, aged 10, is doing a school project on the Battle of Hastings. He knows about Hastings; he went there once whilst on holiday – there's a village called 'Battle'. He remembers a picture of an old tapestry on a postcard; Harold got an arrow in his eye, killed by the Normans, not sure who they were – perhaps something like Romans ...*

(iv) *Jane is an undergraduate student. She knows the Battle of Hastings was the culmination of events in 1066 and a defining moment because the defeat at Hastings, coming after Harold had routed the Vikings in the North, meant that England was destined to be part of Latinised Western Europe rather than the Scandinavian North. She knows that 1066 changed England forever; not that the conflict ended with the Battle of Hastings, the Normans continued to meet resistance – some say traces of the 'Norman Yoke' are still evident in the English class system ...*

How we are to account for these very different instances of knowing that p? The standard characterization would probably run something like this. First, Polly would probably be ruled out as a candidate for knowing that p on grounds that she only has the ability to mimic sounds in response to particular stimuli. Next, it would be acknowledged that Jack, Peter and Jane are certainly very different in terms of what they know, that Peter's knowledge is richer than Jack's, and Jane's richer again. This richness would be characterized partly in quantitative terms – Jane knows *more* things than Peter or Jack – and partly in terms of a 'connectedness' between 'items' of knowledge. Peter, it would be said, has fewer such connections than Jane, and Jack fewer still. 'Rich' or 'real' knowledge, to use Davis's terminology, obtains when items of propositional knowledge are *connected* to other items of knowledge, other facts or propositions.[1]

---

[1] There is a long-standing philosophical debate as to whether propositions are features of language, mind or world. I will not enter into this debate here except to say that the observation that the 'same proposition' can be represented by different sentences (e.g. 'it is raining' and 'il pleut') – usually taken to indicate that propositions must consist in something other than language – is equally consistent with the position to be taken here: that the sentential entities we habitually refer to as propositions are merely contingent manifestations of knowledgeable states.

Within Anglo-American analytic philosophy and philosophy of education, something approximating to this conception of knowledge is hugely prevalent. Yet, there are a number of things about it that should strike us as puzzling. To begin with, given Jack's scant comprehension of dates, history and the like, it might be suggested that his ability to utter '1066' is barely more sophisticated than that of the parrot – he is simply able to respond appropriately to a particular prompt. Are we to say, then, that Jack does not know that p? This might seem odd to someone who had purposefully set out to teach him this fact. If his being able to answer the question correctly is not something he could have done last week, is it unreasonable to want to say that Jack *knows* something he did not know last week? We might try to sidestep this difficulty by saying that Jack has merely developed 'thin knowledge' or a 'thin ability' rather than knowledge proper.[2] Yet, it might then be asked what it is that is required in order that Jack *could* be said to know that p. What does Peter know that enables us to say that he knows that p? If, like Peter, Jack comes to know certain other things, *at what point* could he be said to know that p? Should we not think it strange that in order for a person to be said to know one thing they have to know something else? And, are we to conclude from all this that Jane knows that p *more* than Peter does?

The difficulties don't end there. Let us suppose that Jack does go on to develop appropriate 'connections' with other relevant 'items' of propositional knowledge, say, p^2, p^3, $p^4 \ldots p^n$. Presumably, on this view, we would be obliged to concede that these too, individually and in their unconnected state, must be 'thin'. But, if this is so wherein consists knowledge? It is at this point that we might be inclined to subscribe to some kind of holism. But we need to be clear just how thoroughgoing this holism must be, the sheer extent of the work expected of it. It is not merely that in explaining one 'item' of knowledge we must acknowledge the connections with other 'items'; rather, it is to suggest that each and every 'item' is essentially *constituted* by such connections. This is deeply unsatisfying for any number of reasons. Certainly, we might query the precise nature of

---

[2]In much of his earlier work, Davis contrasts 'rich knowledge' with 'thin *skills*'. See, for example, Davis, 1995.

these connections and ask what it could possibly be for one 'thin' propositional 'item' to be 'connected' to another. But, the essential difficulty is surely this: however much we might be prepared to concede that an epistemic whole could be greater than the sum of its parts, it is difficult to entertain the idea that epistemically vacuous components accrue meaningful content simply by virtue of being 'connected' together.

Now, many would be quick to point out that the obvious and crucial omission from this picture is that of *concepts* and that what is required in order for Jack to be said to *know* that p is that he must come to possess certain relevant concepts – perhaps of historical time and dates, of Hastings as a geographical location, of medieval warfare, and so on. The question, then, is how such concepts stand in relation to propositions. Again, some notion of interconnectedness seems to be called for and many would find quite plausible the kind of quasi-Quinean structure Randall Curren has in mind when in a rejoinder to Davis he asserts with apparent confidence that 'Clusters of beliefs amount to structures of propositions linked to one another through common concepts. One can picture these concepts, *à la* concept maps, as nodes in a web of beliefs' (2006, p. 24). The essential difficulty here is that the notion of 'concept' is no less contentious than that of 'proposition'. But, in the present context, one question is really quite pivotal. Are we to understand concepts *in terms of propositions* or in terms of something else? In other words, are we to think of concepts as consisting solely in the connective or structural features of networks of propositions, or should we regard concepts as introducing another, *different* kind of knowledge or understanding into the picture – knowledge or understanding that is not itself propositional?

On the first view to possess a concept is just to have a certain set of propositional knowledge. Hence, if Jack came to know that the combatants of 1066 used bows and arrows, wore certain types of armour, etc., we might be inclined to say that he had some concept of medieval warfare. Conversely, in the absence of such knowledge, we might wish to deny that Jack has any such concept. Accordingly, on this view, having appropriate propositional knowledge constitutes necessary and sufficient conditions for possessing a concept. It is important to note that this is not merely a point about the evidence needed to attribute the possession of a concept, for even if Jack met with some unfortunate and catastrophic accident which left him incapable of communicating anything of what he knows, it would still be consistent, on this view, to say that his possessing a particular concept is dependent upon him knowing certain kinds of things, that is, propositions of a certain kind. In other words – and any circularity here is stylistic rather than substantive – the point is *conceptual* rather than merely procedural.

The trouble with this notion of concepts is that it does nothing to rid us of our difficulties; it is simply another way of emphasizing the connectedness of propositions. It leaves untouched the question of how it is possible for knowledge to come about from an accumulation of thin propositional 'items'. Of course, there will always be those who feel no need for further explanation, just as there are those who are disposed to accept as unproblematic the idea that 'intelligence' can be created by assembling lines of simple computer code. But, many educators, who often have good cause to distinguish the learner's capacity to trade propositions from knowledge proper, are likely to harbour at least a suspicion that it is logically possible for someone to have a substantial array of propositional 'knowledge' at their disposal whilst not knowing very much at all.

We thus turn to the other possibility, the idea that to possess a 'concept' is to possess something that is epistemologically and logically distinct from any proposition or ostensible 'network' of propositions. On this view, to possess a concept is to possess something that renders us capable of giving meaningful content to propositions, of interpreting them and using them in appropriate ways. In a word, concepts can be conceived of as providing us with the means to *understand* that which comes to us in propositional form. Now, this reading of 'concepts' removes at a stroke the problem of how it is possible for thin propositional entities to constitute rich knowledge. Rich knowledge, we might say, consists of propositions *plus* concepts. To say this is not to be committed to positing the existence of any specific, identifiably discrete mental entities. We may wish to do no more than acknowledge that knowledge proper requires *something more* than just propositions. Yet, we may already begin to suspect that this 'something more', whether we refer to it as 'concepts' or prefer to use some other term, must constitute the more fundamental and perhaps more substantial part of knowledge. And it is thus that if *this* is what we mean when we speak of 'concepts' – and it would seem that this is the only way that we can lend any credibility to this picture – then we are obliged to concede that it is concepts, rather than propositions, which are of greater epistemic and educational import and in the context of the present discussion more deserving of philosophic attention. We might say that if this is what is meant by 'concepts', then there is an important sense in which in focusing on propositions we are attending to the *wrong thing*.

Of course, there are terms other than 'concept' which may serve us better, not least because 'concepts' carries an implicit assumption of the possibility of individuation. To speak of 'conceptual understanding' or just 'understanding' would at least avoid this difficulty. There are potential pitfalls here too if we allow ourselves to think of 'understanding' as something *applied to* knowledge. We must remain resolute that what we are trying to get clear about *is* knowledge. A notion such as 'Background', as John Searle has used it, would perhaps not be inappropriate for our purposes. Searle demonstrates the sheer epistemic and cognitive extent of what is at issue when he considers what is involved in our understanding a simple sentence such as 'She gave him her key and he opened the door'.

> There is much discussion about whether when a speaker utters that sentence it is actually said (or merely implied) that he opened the door *with that key*, and whether he actually says that she *first* gave him the key and *then later* he opened the door; but it is generally agreed that there is a certain underdetermination of what is said by the literal meaning of the sentence. I wish to say that there is a *radical* underdetermination of what is said by the literal meaning of the sentence. There is nothing in the literal meaning of the sentence 'She gave him her key and he opened the door' to block the interpretation, He opened the door with her key by bashing the door down with the key; the key weighed two hundred pounds and was in the shape of an axe. Or, He swallowed both the door and the key and he inserted the key in the lock by the peristaltic contraction of his gut. (original emphases; Searle, 1995, p. 131)

As Searle says, it is possible to imagine any number of possible and possibly outlandish interpretations for this or any other sentence. The only reason such interpretations would normally be 'blocked' is that we have 'a certain sort of knowledge about how the world works' (Searle, 1995), a 'Background' of 'capacities, dispositions, know-how, etc., which are not themselves part of the semantic content of the sentence' (p. 130). For our purposes, the vital thing here is the way in which this diminishes the status of propositions quite dramatically in the epistemic and cognitive scheme of things: there is an important sense in which propositions *qua* propositions don't mean very much at all. We might even ask whether Searle's characterization is 'radical' enough, that is, whether propositions have *any* integral epistemic substance, whether somehow *all* of their content derives from the Background. But, the essential thing here is the way in which such considerations would seem to undermine the assumption that knowledge consists of propositions. Knowledge proper, it would seem, is that which lies behind any given proposition or ostensible 'structure' of propositions.

All things considered the interconnected knowledge thesis looks increasingly untenable. First, by Davis's own account we are obliged to concede that in and of itself the holding of a proposition amounts at best to 'thin' knowledge; second, we can only sustain the idea of knowledge as interconnected propositions by transferring the epistemic work to some other notion such as 'concepts'; finally, it would appear that propositional utterances are largely if not entirely dependent for their meaning on a form of understanding that is essentially non-propositional. Such considerations seem to demand a different characterization of propositions and their relationship to knowledge.

An altogether more feasible alternative, I want to suggest, is to regard propositions not as components of knowledge but, rather, as *manifestations* of knowledge. That propositions *are* manifest in the form of utterances and written sentences is trivially true. What I am proposing is that we go wrong when we assume the existence of some directly corresponding epistemic entity – something 'in the head', so to speak. Of course, knowledge can be manifest in other than propositional form: performances and behaviours other than the issuing of propositions. Indeed, this alone should be sufficient to alert us to the shortcomings of the interconnected knowledge thesis. But the key thing here is that that it would seem that knowledge is *never* equivalent to its manifestations. To adopt Searle's way of speaking, we might say that there is *always* a radical under-determination of knowledge by its manifestations.

Now, it seems to me that our distinguishing knowledge from its manifestations in this way allows a far more coherent explanation of what our four individuals know. We are able to acknowledge that what each of them knows, each of their doxastic states, is very different; it just happens that each is such as can give rise to the very same outward manifestation, the same propositional utterance. We can thus relinquish the idea that knowledge has discernible parts. Certainly, we can distinguish one manifestation from another and we can also identify broad categories of manifestation – which is precisely what we do when, for example, we distinguish between 'knowing how' and 'knowing that'. But it would seem that when knowledge is distinguished from its outward manifestations we lack grounds to regard it as anything other than an amorphous and undifferentiated doxastic whole. In this sense, we could say that the entirety of what we know is 'interconnected' – but not because we can feasibly posit the existence of discrete but somehow 'connected' items of knowledge, but rather, because knowledge cannot feasibly be conceived as comprised of separate, distinct entities in the first place. Try counting how many beliefs you have. The reason this is impossible is precisely because what we know can be manifest in a virtually infinite number of ways, in other words, potentially any number of 'beliefs' couched in propositional form.

The upshot of this, I think, is that it is necessary to distinguish two very different ways of thinking about 'knowledge' in relation to education. In the context of teaching, curriculum design and so on, it is entirely feasible to conceive of knowledge in terms of inner knowledgeable states. Any genuine instance of teaching should surely be informed by an implicit understanding of what it is to know the thing in question. It is not without significance that we invariably have difficulty articulating this in any precise terms, but what we *can* describe are the processes likely to foster such knowledge. The pedagogical strategies we come to adopt should properly be informed by our understanding of what it is to know and we can conceive of this in as 'rich' or as 'thin' a sense as happens to suit our purposes. To return to our previous examples, we would presume that Jane's tutor would have a keen sense of the 'rich' knowledge he hopes Jane will develop in reading for her degree. And by the same token, the person who trains Polly the parrot will have a certain conception of knowledge in mind, albeit one that occasions a very different and obviously far more limited educational project. From this perspective, then, from the perspective of *teaching*, we can distinguish different senses of what it is to know and recognize that there is a world of difference between teaching someone to 'parrot' the facts and teaching someone to have the kind of knowledge we might associate with a university education.

However, in the context of assessment, where the task is the very different one of *determining* what a person knows, it is a rather different matter. Our patent lack of access to the contents of other minds means that our judgements about what other people know *must* ultimately derive from the outward, evident manifestations of knowledge. There is thus an important sense in which when we speak of a person's knowledge in the context of assessment we mean something rather different from what we mean when we refer to knowledge in the context of teaching or curriculum design. The difficulties that arise when these two meanings are confused are all too familiar. Those who conceive of teaching and curriculum in terms of knowledge's evident manifestations will err towards a cognitively impoverished, behaviouristic conception of the educational enterprise. Conversely, those who rightly recognize the inadequacies of a curriculum couched in terms of knowledge's outward manifestations will go wrong when they apply the same measure to the processes of assessment – processes that are *necessarily* focused on the manifestations of knowledge – and condemn those processes for being focused on 'thin skills' or 'thin knowledge' as opposed to 'rich', 'real' or 'genuine' knowledge. The danger then is that the viability of *all* assessment is undermined. And it is just this conflation which is evident in Davis's contrast of 'rich', 'interconnected' knowledge on the one hand, and 'thin' knowledge 'that I can only use to answer an appropriately phrased question' (p. 12) on the other. This, I want to suggest, is what has caused Davis's critics to see in his argument a pervasive scepticism towards the very possibility of meaningful assessment. But the main point here is that if we are to get clearer about what is wrong with using assessment to hold schools and teachers account, then *pace* Davis we need to abandon the idea that this is about the kind of knowledge we choose to assess, whether it is thin or rich, discrete or interconnected. As we will see, the distinction that is more substantively at issue turns out not to relate to knowledge at all but to the evidence we have of a person's knowledge, or more exactly, what it is we *do* with that evidence.

Two concepts of assessment

Part of the appeal of criterion-referenced assessment is its apparent simplicity. Criteria specify what a person should know or should be able to do and assessment is configured to determine whether they *do* know or whether they *can* do. Yet, this apparent simplicity disguises the fact – one which seems to have been completely overlooked in current thinking about assessment – that whenever we set out to discover what a person knows or is capable of we have at our disposal two logically distinct and parallel approaches.

By way of illustration consider how a teacher in an informal classroom situation might judge her pupil not to understand despite his answering her question correctly, or conversely, judge that he *does* understand despite answering incorrectly. If asked to explain this, the teacher would probably describe it as a case in which the pupil's outward behaviour is at odds with his 'inner' capabilities, with what he 'really' knows. Yet, the plain fact is that the teacher has no access to the pupil's inner knowledgeable states. The distinction here, I want to suggest, is not between the 'inner' and the 'outer' but, rather, between one particular instance of the pupil's behaviour and the 'picture' the teacher has of that pupil and his capabilities, construed from whatever evidence she has gleaned and has deemed to be significant.

There is a wealth of empirical evidence in the psychology of perception to support the thesis that we construct such 'pictures' for each and every person we come to know, and that we do this by engaging in profoundly complex and largely unconscious processes of judgement which involve interpreting and selecting from the evidence available to us (see Lum, 2012). Returning to our previous vignette for a moment, suppose we had been told that all the respondents answered '1066' except for Jane who answered '1067'. What would we make of this? We might wonder whether her answer was a slip of the tongue. Was she perhaps making a joke? Could it be that she has been persuaded by some recent research which raised doubts about the true date of the battle? There again, were we mistaken in assuming that she is reading for a degree in history? What if we learnt that she is in fact studying chemistry and knows next to nothing about history – she just happened to memorize a few facts for the exercise? The point here is that even with these imaginary characters, sketched in a just few lines of text, we are automatically disposed to construe something of the 'person' from the few clues available to us, however subtle or brief these might be. We thus get an inkling of the unconscious and automatic nature of the resources we bring to bear in our attempts to understand what other people know.

It would seem that in our ordinary dealings with people we continually compare instances of a person's behaviour with the picture we have of that person, constantly updating and modifying that picture as we are presented with more detailed or more recent information. The upshot, in effect, is that we alternate between two kinds of judgement: one by which we determine whether a given instance of behaviour is of a particular type (e.g. 'he answered the question correctly'), and another by which we draw on *any* evidence we see fit in order to construct a picture of the person and their capabilities which influences reflexively our understanding of any particular instance of behaviour (e.g. 'but he didn't *really* understand'). This natural bifurcation in our facility to understand what other people know, think, believe, feel and so on would seem to be of vital importance in our dealings with other human beings and is fundamental to the business of teaching. But more important here are the implications of this for *formal* assessment procedures, implications which seem not merely to have escaped notice but to have been almost systematically misrepresented in theorizing about assessment.

We get a sense of these implications in the following thought experiment, what I have called the 'Right/Wrong Scenario':

> Imagine that we wished to assess a person's knowledge of, say, current affairs by means of oral questioning. And suppose that this person was able to answer our questions correctly but with each and every answer betrayed some either quite subtle or perhaps quite radical misunderstanding. Perhaps on being asked who the current British Prime Minister is the response comes 'David Cameron – leader of the Liberal Democrats', or 'David Cameron – the Welshman who lives at No 9 Downing Street', or 'David Cameron – a lizard-like alien from Mars who lives in the sewers of New York'. Let us say, then, that with each and every 'correct' answer comes countervailing evidence which suggests that the respondent does not fully understand the matter in hand.... The question here is whether and in what sense there could be said to be a correct or appropriate interpretation of such a response. (Lum, 2012, p. 596)

Now in the previous culture of psychometric testing, a culture of 'constructs' and 'universes' of potential test items, this might appear at first sight not to pose any real difficulty. On this view, if it matters to us whether the respondent does or does not know that David Cameron is leader of the Conservative Party, we need only include an extra test question to that effect. However, the fact that it is logically possible for the Right/Wrong Scenario to obtain *however many questions are set* might give us cause for doubt as to the extent to which the statistical artefacts which result from psychometric assessment could be said to capture what it is a person actually does or does not know. What is still more to the point, however, is that the option of adding further questions is no solution at all in the context of criterion-referenced or competence/outcomes-based assessment where we are concerned only with determining whether a person does or does not know the thing in question. It is in this context that it would seem that we have to *choose* between two logically distinct approaches, between the two kinds of judgement by which we ordinarily make sense of what people know.

Let us suppose, for example, that this scenario occurred in the context of a door-to-door survey of prospective voters. Here, we could presume that the role of the 'assessor' would be to confirm whether the respondent is able to make a certain response, it having been determined in advance that the responses 'David Cameron' or 'Mr Cameron' are to be deemed 'correct'. The 'assessor' has no interest in anything beyond this hence the responses given would automatically merit a tick in the relevant box – the respondent *did* know that David Cameron is the Prime Minister. In contrast, if this same scenario occurred in the context of an MP using the very same questions to assess applicants for an internship at Westminster, it seems inconceivable that such responses could do other than result in a negative outcome. In each case, the *same* questions are posed, the *same* answers are sought and exactly the *same* responses are received, yet in each case, there is an entirely different outcome. And it would clearly not be sufficient – even though it is obviously true – to account for this by saying that each 'assessor' has different purposes. The essential difference between the two approaches, I want to suggest, is not their different purposes but the stance each takes *towards the evidence*.

It would seem that with any formal process intended to determine whether a person does or does not know *x* or can or cannot do *y* we have to make a determinate choice between the two approaches. Elsewhere (Lum, 2012), I have referred to these as *prescriptive* and *expansive* modes of assessment, with each mode employing a particular kind of judgement. In the prescriptive mode, an assessor employs *judgements of identity* to determine, in essentially binary fashion, whether certain predetermined and rigidly prescribed manifestations are in evidence or not. In contrast, in the *expansive mode*, an assessor will employ what I have called *judgements of significance*, the assessor being at liberty to expand the focus of their attention to take account of *any* available evidence and evaluate the significance of that evidence as he or she sees fit.

Now, as I have said, we apply both these kinds of judgement quite naturally in our everyday dealings with people. It is when these judgements are conceived of in the context of formalized assessment procedures that the difference between them is often misunderstood. In assessment circles, what I have referred to here as judgements of significance in the expansive mode will often be described using terms such as 'holistic', 'inferential', 'impressionistic' or 'aesthetic'. Critics of current assessment arrangements can often be seen to employ characterizations of this kind to highlight the subjective, tentative or contestable nature of such judgements, the intention being to show that such judgements cannot provide the level of 'objectivity' assumed by these arrangements. Whilst the intention might in part be justified, the difficulty with characterizations of this kind is that they suggest a process that is fundamentally unreliable, even arbitrary. And, again, this seems to suggest that there is cause to be sceptical about the possibility of meaningful assessment. Yet, it is clear from our example of the MP faced with the Right/ Wrong Scenario that this is simply not the case. We would certainly not dismiss the MP's judgement on grounds of being 'subjective' or 'arbitrary'. What distinguishes the mode of assessment used in the door-to-door survey from that used by the MP is that whilst the former is confined to rigidly prescribed manifestations the latter makes use of the fullest range of evidence available. Seen thus, the process employed by the MP would be acknowledged to provide the *better* indication of what the candidate knows.

The advantage of assessment in the prescriptive mode is that it allows us to acknowledge specific performances irrespective of wider circumstances, and as such, it provides highly commensurable results and fine-grained comparability between candidates or groups of candidates (e.g. schools). The advantage of assessment in the expansive mode is that it allows the assessor to draw on the fullest range of evidence to construe, in effect, 'a picture' of the person and their capabilities and thus make the best possible estimation of what it is they know or can do. It is significant that in the event of the two modes being at variance the expansive mode will almost always trump the prescriptive mode – cheating in an exam being a case in point. But, the expansive mode has one major drawback in that the assessor's estimation of what a candidate knows can only be made commensurable with estimations of what other candidates know by being articulated in the broadest and most equivocal of terms.

In the design of any formal assessment, a clear decision *has* to be made which mode to employ because, as the Right/Wrong Scenario demonstrates, the outcome of any assessment could well depend on the mode employed. It is thus vital for reasons of consistency and fairness that a determinate choice be made as to an assessment's intended mode. A determinate and transparent choice has to be made between, on the one hand, a mode of assessment that allows fine-grained comparability, and on the other, a mode of assessment that affords the best possible estimation of knowledge, but which can only be made commensurable, and thus comparable, in the most equivocal of terms. There can be no halfway house between the two modes: either the requisite manifestations are specified in advance in the manner of the prescriptive mode, or arrangements are such as to allow the assessor to operate freely in the expansive mode. And, this brings us to the question of what is wrong with using assessment to hold schools and teachers to account.

The paradox of assessment for accountability

It is precisely when the stakes are high, when there is an obligation to achieve the very best estimation of knowledge, that it becomes imperative to employ assessment in the expansive mode. To see why, consider again the examples of high-stakes testing cited by Randall Curren (2006). In his critical rejoinder to Davis, Curren makes much of the fact that we can and do use assessment with acceptable levels of reliability in high-stakes situations. In this he is certainly correct. The important thing, however, is the *kind* of assessment that is used. The assessment of a defendant's guilt or innocence in a court of law certainly has high stakes. It also epitomizes assessment in the expansive mode. The court will consider *all* available and relevant evidence and weigh the significance of that evidence in order to determine whether there was criminal intent – that is, *mens rea* (literally guilty mind). It is not insignificant that when the stakes are relatively low as with, say, a parking offence, a prosecution might typically proceed on the basis of the *actus reus* (guilty act) alone: the fact that a person's car was parked in such a way as to contravene the regulations, regardless of circumstances, is sufficient basis for a prosecution. In other words, the process will be characteristic of assessment in the prescriptive mode. But, it is also significant that even here, *when it really matters*, there will almost invariably be the opportunity to have recourse to expansive mode type procedures, the opportunity to put before the court *all* of the evidence and to have the court give due consideration to the full significance of that evidence.

Similarly, with Curren's other example: the assessment of medical students' fitness to practice. It is inconceivable that this could be done by assessment in the prescriptive mode. It is true that medical training, like other areas of professional and vocational education, has not been immune to the encroaching tide of 'competences', 'outcomes' and other such similar accoutrements which more often than not will be seen to have the characteristic features of prescriptive mode assessment. Yet, however much these kinds of procedures might be made a necessary condition of fitness to practice, they could never be deemed *sufficient* condition. Those who would assume otherwise might be challenged to set out the criteria sufficient to indicate fitness for practice, a list of test items or can do's such that any person who might walk in off the street and who could meet such criteria – regardless of training, education or experience – could with confidence be deemed fit to practice. The very idea, of course, is preposterous. Prescriptive mode assessment is inadequate for *any* high-stakes purposes and its use for such purposes is bound to have unacceptable consequences. The fact is that when it is essential to make the very best estimation of knowledge – and evaluating teachers and schools is a case in point – assessment *must* be in the expansive mode.

The obvious question here is which of the two modes is used in our schools? Given that this is essentially an empirical question and given also that the distinction I have made here between prescriptive and expansive forms of assessment goes unacknowledged in the current scheme of things, then strictly speaking we simply don't know. But, it seems certain that SATs (Standard Assessment Tests) will generally have the characteristics and hence limitations of prescriptive mode assessment. Which mode is adopted for teacher assessment is a more complex matter. The thing most likely to influence the choice of mode is the form that descriptors, criteria, statements of attainment, etc., take. For example, if a teacher was required to determine whether a certain piece of a child's writing contained 'recognisable letters', 'time-related words' or a 'sequence of events' (QCA, 2007, p. 23), she would presumably adopt the binary methods of the prescriptive mode, the task being one of determining whether or not the features specified appear in the child's writing. On the other hand, if she was required to determine whether the child is able to 'write imaginative, interesting and thoughtful texts' (QCA, 2007), it is likely, all things being equal, that she would adopt the methods of the expansive mode, that is she would be inclined to consider and afford significance to any available evidence. It is of interest to note here the implicit (and unwitting) suggestion by the assessment designers that the focus of attention in the first case should be on the child's writing, and in the second, on the child's 'ability'. Of course, the substantive issue is not whether we are concerned with outward behaviours/performances as against 'inner' abilities or states; rather, it is a matter of the stance the assessor is required to take towards the evidence. But, the main point here is that criteria specifying manifest behaviours or outcomes will invariably prompt assessment in the prescriptive mode while criteria specifying attributes of the person will most likely prompt assessment in the expansive mode.

We can expect any ambiguity on this score to give rise to all too familiar complaints from those tasked with carrying out the assessment. Those anticipating the clear-cut procedures of the prescriptive mode will regard criteria in the expansive mode as impracticably vague: 'But what do they *mean*?' will be the cry. Conversely, those who would instinctively adopt the methods of the expansive mode will decry procedures in the prescriptive mode which, as they see it, require them to record results in the face of contrary indications and against their better judgement. And, the matter is *not*, as might commonly be supposed, one of degree, a matter of more or less tightly specified criteria indicating more or less tightly specified assessment. When it comes to the role of the assessor, there is a simple and straightforward choice between the two modes.

However, things are not quite as straightforward as this might seem to suggest, and we begin to get a sense of the potential complications when we note that in point of fact *all* the criteria indicated above come from *one* single assessment item in the

QCAs *Teachers Handbook for Writing* (Levels 1–3). The ability to 'write imaginative, interesting and thoughtful texts' is styled as an 'assessment focus' which is then cashed out in terms of a requirement to determine whether the child's writing contains such things as 'recognisable letters', 'time-related words' and a 'sequence of events'. In other words, a descriptor which appears at first sight to be such as might prompt assessment in the expansive mode turns out to have no role in the assessment process at all!

What we can say with some certainty is that demands for commensurable and auditable evidence will almost invariably prompt assessment in the prescriptive as opposed to the expansive mode. In other words, assessors will be confined to the evidence specified and be obliged to disregard any other indications. Even where criteria appear quite unambiguous in indicating procedures in the expansive mode, it is entirely possible that through processes of 'training' or 'moderation', under the guise of establishing 'agreed interpretations', assessors will ultimately be steered towards assessment in the prescriptive mode.

We can thus begin to see the paradox at the centre of this whole issue. To employ assessment in the expansive mode is always, ultimately, to place trust in the assessor's judgement. But, when trust is precisely that which is at issue, as it is when assessment is intended to measure the effectiveness of educators and educational institutions, then it is inevitable that judgements made in this mode will appear unacceptably ambiguous and lacking in substance. When political and managerial distrust is combined with the philosophically naïve demand to know *exactly* what children know, then it is inevitable that assessment will come to be conceived in the prescriptive mode – the very mode that is profoundly and irredeemably incompatible with *any* high-stakes purpose. The bureaucratic compulsion for specificity and commensurability thus becomes self-defeating, because any intervention designed to circumvent the judgements of those carrying out the assessment will invariably conflict with the ambition to determine what children actually know and what schools and teachers have achieved. Paradoxically, the strategies which would best serve this ambition, the strategies which would naturally be employed in any other circumstance, any other walk of life, are unfeasible for the purpose of assessing schools and teachers because the only people able to carry out such assessment are, ultimately, the very people being assessed.

Against this background, Davis's points about inspection are entirely pertinent. What has been said here about assessment applies equally to inspection: the process of inspection must similarly draw on one or other of these two forms of judgement. And, whilst judgements of identity in the prescriptive mode will usefully allow checks to be made on such things as timetabling or the existence of appropriate school policies, inspectors will be greatly impeded in their facility to make meaningful judgements in the expansive mode. As Davis rightly says, any inspector by virtue of being an 'outside observer' (p. 47) will have access only to 'limited evidence' (p. 48); accordingly, they will be profoundly limited in their capacity to apply judgements of significance in the expansive mode, the kind of judgements which are needed if a proper estimation of schools and teachers is to be made.

But the difficulty is not merely that current arrangements are unable to provide a fair or reasonable indication of the achievements of schools and teachers, though this alone is serious enough. Rather – and it is this intuition which is surely at the heart of Davis's argument – it is that they are likely to be of profound detriment to education. To see why, it is necessary to recognize a sense of 'teaching to the test' that is rather different from how this expression is ordinarily understood. Of course, in the previous culture of psychometrics – a culture of 'constructs' and sampling from 'universes' of potential test items – 'teaching to the test' meant purposefully teaching those elements selected or likely to be selected for the test. The remedy for this, as everyone knows, is unseen examinations. But, in the new culture of assessing what a person actually knows or can do, any such selection is incidental: the process is intended expressly to determine whether the learner does or does not know the things that have been identified as worth teaching. In this scheme of things, 'teaching to the test' is a virtue – it is what is expected of the teacher. However, in light of the present discussion, a very different sense of 'teaching to the test' arises with the possibility that teaching could be contrived in such a way as to instil behaviours or understandings that would be sufficient to meet the requirements of the prescriptive mode, but which would not be sufficient for assessment in the expansive mode. This corresponds closely with Davis's concern about rote learning. The difference between us is that whilst for Davis the problem centres on assessing 'thin knowledge' as opposed to 'rich knowledge', in contrast, what I am suggesting is that the essential difficulty turns on the *evidence* required for assessment and the stance the assessor is required to take towards that evidence. If prescriptive mode assessment is used for accountability purposes, then the immediate interests of schools and teachers, in contrast to the interests of learners, would seem to be best served by conceiving of teaching and learning in terms sufficient only to meet the requirements of assessment in the prescriptive as opposed to the expansive mode.

None of this is to say that there is no place for prescriptive mode assessment in education, not least because this mode of assessment – we might think of a simple spelling test, for example – clearly has an important role in informing the expansive mode type judgements teachers need to make as part of the process of teaching. But, when detached from such a context, when used not to supplement but to circumvent the teacher's judgement, its effect is always to subjugate substantive educational ends to other ends. At root, the essential difficulty is that it *requires* the assessor to disregard evidence which might indicate more properly what a person knows. Just as in the case of the door-to-door survey, in the event that the respondent in the Right/Wrong Scenario believes that David Cameron is a lizard-like alien from Mars, then not only must this fact go unrecognized but so too must the need for educational (or psychiatric) intervention. Used thus, as an end in itself rather than as a means to an end, the prescriptive mode is antithetical to substantive educational concerns, at odds with our most fundamental educational instincts.

It would seem that for several decades our use of terms such as 'criteria', 'competences', outcomes' etc., has served to conceal the fact that whenever we set out to determine whether a person does or does not know a specific thing we have no option but to choose, even if unwittingly, between two fundamentally different processes of assessment. Both are essential to the business of teaching and learning, and Winch is certainly correct in acknowledging assessment to be an integral and indispensable part of the process of education. Our distinguishing between these two modes does nothing to detract from the possibility of meaningful assessment and its important place in education. Yet, neither mode, for different reasons, can properly be used for accountability purposes. On the one hand, assessment in the prescriptive mode is demonstrably inadequate for any high-stakes purpose and when used to hold schools and teachers to account places the interests of schools and teachers at odds with the interests of learners. When assessment is in this mode, then, as Davis has rightly recognized, it will invariably tend to distort the processes of teaching and learning. On the other hand, assessment in the expansive mode, the kind of assessment that in any other context *would* be appropriate for high-stakes purposes, is manifestly unfeasible for holding schools and teachers to account, first, because it cannot provide the requisite comparability, and second, because it would require of those who commission such procedures the one thing that, ultimately, is most fundamentally at issue: that is, trust. This, I want to suggest, is the essential difficulty with using assessment to hold schools and teachers to account.

Do we need to rethink criterion-referenced and competence/outcome-based assessment?

The comprehensive and widespread shift in assessment methodology over the past two or three decades towards forms of assessment variously identified as criterion-referenced or competence/outcome-based has attracted no small amount of criticism. The fact that such procedures now predominate in so many areas of education in so many different parts of the world testifies to the failure of that criticism to gain any substantial purchase on the policy and practice of educational assessment.

A recurring theme in the critical response to competence/outcome-based assessment in vocational and professional education – a context in which a concern for 'doing' might be thought entirely appropriate – is the complaint that such methods, in attending primarily to what a person can do, in effect subscribe to a form of behaviourism and are thus intrinsically neglectful of knowledge and understanding (see Hyland, 1994). Advocates of these approaches are generally unmoved: if the point of vocational/ professional education is to enable to people to act in a certain capacity, then what can possibly be wrong with assessment designed to determine if they *can* perform in that capacity? If candidates are able to demonstrate the requisite behaviour, then, fluke performances aside, we can surely take it that they *do* have the wherewithal as regards knowledge, understanding or indeed anything else that is required. The standard riposte from critics is that whilst the knowledge and understanding a person possesses might be sufficient in *one* context, it might not be sufficient in another. In other words, if we fail to attend specifically to knowledge and understanding, then the learner may prove *not* to be competent if or when required to perform in a different context. Indeed, we can recall how Andrew Davis makes just this sort of point in relation to the 'transfer' (p. 14) of knowledge from one context to another. However, if it is then claimed that the ability in question *is* tested across a sufficient range of contexts, the critic would seem to be left struggling to provide any basis for his complaint.

Now, in light of the present discussion, I think it is possible to offer a rather different analysis of the problem and a rather different characterization of the anxiety that many have long had about competence/outcome-based assessment. It should be clear by now that designations such as 'competence-based' and 'outcome-based' are not sufficient. What is more to the point is whether the arrangements at issue are characteristic of prescriptive or expansive mode assessment. And again, strictly speaking this is an empirical matter, although there is every reason to believe that much of the UK system of Scottish/National Vocational Qualifications (S/NVQs) would be more correctly identified as erring towards prescriptive mode assessment. But I want to suggest that the anxiety many have had long about these arrangements should more properly be seen as stemming from an implicit recognition that an assessor operating in the prescriptive mode could find themselves being required to acknowledge competence *in the face of countervailing evidence* – precisely as illustrated by the Right/ Wrong Scenario.

Again, this is not to say that there is no place for prescriptive mode procedures in vocational and professional education for besides any formative worth they might have, such procedures have an important role in informing the expansive mode judgements that *should* be used to determine a person's fitness to practice. So neither is this to suggest that we should abandon the focus on competence to return to the previous testing culture where too much reliance was placed on the testing of theory. What it does mean, however, is that we should recognize the profound limitations of assessment in the prescriptive mode and the importance of judgements in the expansive mode. Given the high stakes often associated with assessing competence, it will often be imperative to draw on as wide a range of evidence as possible, extending far beyond the immediate confines of the workplace to take full account of a person's education and experience. This will be an anathema to many competence strategists who automatically and unwittingly conceive of 'competences' and 'outcomes' in prescriptive terms. Of course, in having an eye to the kind of training or education a person has had, it would seem necessary to have an indication of the extent to which that process is likely to have contributed to the learner's understanding. In this volume, Christopher Winch usefully draws attention to the variety of purposes of assessment and there is perhaps one more use of assessment that we might add to this taxonomy. For one somewhat paradoxical consequence of conceiving of competence assessment in the expansive mode is that would seem to suggest that pen and paper tests, unseen examinations and the like, might be repositioned in the scheme of things – the purpose of such tests being not to demonstrate knowledge per se but to provide an indication of the effectiveness of the processes of learning to which the learner has been exposed.

This by no means answers all the questions likely to be raised in connection with the use of expansive mode assessment in vocational and professional settings. There will be questions about trust and the need for checks and balances, questions about what count as a sufficiency of evidence, and so on. But the main thing here is that we certainly stand in need of a radical rethink as regards the arrangements we stereotypically designate as 'criterion-referenced', 'competence-based' or 'outcome-based'. It is plainly no longer sufficient to say that such arrangements simply determine whether a person knows x, or can do y.

Bibliography

Aristotle (1925) *Nichomachean Ethics* (David Ross edition), London, Dent.

Assessment of Performance Unit (1985) *A Review of Monitoring in Mathematics 1978 to 1982* (2 vols), London, DES.

Baker, G. P. and Hacker, P. M. S. (1985) *Rules, Grammar and Necessity*, Oxford, Blackwell.

BBC (2011a) *Government to Phase out Modular GCSEs from 2012*, http://www.bbc.co.uk/news/education-13922439 (last accessed 29 July 2014)

———. (2011b) *Reading Check for Six-Year-Olds Rolled Out*, http://www.bbc.co.uk/news/education-14930193 (last accessed 29 July 2014).

———. (2011c) *Schools 'Pushed into Phonics by Financial Incentives'*, http://www.bbc.co.uk/news/education-14029897 (last accessed 29 July 2014).

———. (2012) *CBI Complains of 'Exam Factory' Schools*, http://www.bbc.co.uk/news/education-20355664 (last accessed 29 July 2014).

Bengson, J. and Moffett, M. A. (2007) Know-How and Concept Possession, *Philosophical Studies*, 136, pp. 31–57.

———. (2011) Non-Propositional Intellectualism, in J. Bengson and M. A. Moffett (eds) *Knowing How, Essays on Knowledge, Mind and Action*, Oxford, OUP, pp. 161–195.

Black, P. (1994) Performance Assessment and Accountability: The Experience in England and Wales, *Educational Evaluation and Policy Analysis*, 16, 2, pp. 191–203.

Black, P. and Wiliam, D. (2001) *Inside the Black Box BERA Short Final Draft*, http://weaeducation.typepad.co.uk/files/blackbox-1.pdf

———. (2006) The Reliability of Assessments, in J. Gardner (ed.) *Assessment and Learning*, London, Sage Publications, pp. 119–131.

Brown, M. (1991) Problematic Issues in National Assessment, *Cambridge Journal of Education*, 21, 2, pp. 215–229.

———. (2010) Are We Getting Better at Educating? Department of Education and Professional Studies, King's College, London Annual Lecture.

Burgess, S., Wilson, D. and Worth, J. (October 2010), *A Natural Experiment in School Accountability: The Impact of School*

Performance Information on Pupil Progress and Sorting, The Centre For Market And Public Organisation, Working Paper No. 10/246.

Butler, T. and Webber, R. (2007) Classifying Pupils by Where They Live: How Well Does This Predict Variations in Their GCSE Results?, *Urban Studies*, 44, 7, pp. 1229–1253.

Campbell, D. (1976). *Assessing the Impact of Planned Social Change*, The Public Affairs Center, Dartmouth College, Hanover, NH.

Carraher, D. and Schliemann, A. (2002) The Transfer Dilemma, *The Journal of the Learning Sciences*, 77, 1, pp. 1–24.

Ceci, S. J. (1996) *On Intelligence...More or Less: A bio-Ecological Treatise on Intellectual Development*, Englewood Cliffs, NJ, Prentice-Hall.

Ceci, S. J. and Roazzi, A. (1994) The Effects of Context on Cognition: Postcards from Brazil, in R. J. Sternberg and R. K. Wagner (eds) *Mind in Context: Interactionist Perspectives on Human Intelligence*, New York, NY, Cambridge University Press.

Chudgar, A. and Quin, E. (2012) The Relationship between Private Schooling and Achievement: Results from Rural and Urban India, *Economics of Education Review*, 4, p. 376–390.

Coles, M. (2007) *Qualifications Frameworks in Europe: Platforms for Qualifications, Integration and Reform*, Brussels, EU, Education and Culture DG (last accessed 9 March 2014).

Curren, R. (2006) Connected Learning and the Foundations of Psychometrics: A Rejoinder, *Journal of Philosophy of Education*, 40, 1, pp. 1–16.

Davis, A. (1995) Criterion-Referenced Assessment and the Development of Knowledge and Understanding, *Journal of Philosophy of Education*, 29, 1, pp. 3–22.

———. (1988) Ability and Learning, *Journal of Philosophy of Education*, 22, 1, pp. 45–55.

———. (1999) Prescribing Teaching Methods, *Journal of Philosophy of Education*, 33, 3, pp. 387–401.

———. (2010) An apple for the Inspector *Questa* 1. http://www2.warwick.ac.uk/fac/soc/pais/people/swift/publications/questa_complete.pdf

———. (2012) A Monstrous Regimen of Synthetic Phonics: Fantasies of Research-Based Teaching 'Methods' Versus Real Teaching. *Journal of Philosophy of Education* 46, 4 pp. 560–573.

———. (2013) *To Read or Not to Read: Decoding Synthetic Phonics Impact No. 20*, Philosophy of Education Society of Great Britain, London.

Davis, A. and Cigman, R. (2008) Commentary, in A. Davis and R. Cigman (eds) *New Philosophies of Learning*, Oxford, Wiley, pp.705–707.

Dearden, R. F. (1984) The Assessment of Learning, in *Theory and Practice in Education*, London, Routledge, pp. 123–137.

Department of Education and Science (1987) Task Group on Assessment and Testing (TGAT) report, Department of Education and Science and the Welsh Office.

DFE (1995a) *Science in the National Curriculum*, London, HMSO.

———. (1995b) *English in the National Curriculum*, London, HMSO.

———. (1995c) *Mathematics in the National Curriculum*, London, HMSO.

———. (2011a) *The Importance of Teaching: Schools White Paper*, http://www.education.gov.uk/b0068570/the-importance-of-teaching/accountability/minimum-standard-for-every-school

———. (2011b) *Training Our Next Generation of Outstanding Teachers*, London, HMSO.

DfEE (1998) *Teaching: High Status, High Standards*, Circular 4/98 London, HMSO.

———. (2006) *Primary National Strategy*, London, HMSO http://www.standards.dfes.gov.uk/primary/features/primary/pri_fwk_corepapers/pri_fwk_corepapers_0385506.pdf

Dwyer, J. G. (2004) School Accountability and 'High Stakes' Testing, *Theory and Research in Education*, 2, 3, pp. 211–217.

Ellenbogen, S. (2003) *Wittgenstein's Account of Truth*, Albany, State University of New York Press.

Everitt, N. and Fisher, A. (1995) *Modern Epistemology*, London, McGraw Hill.

Everson, K., Feinauer, E. and Sudweeks, R. (2013) Rethinking Teacher Evaluation: A Conversation about Statistical Inferences and Value-Added Models, *Harvard Educational Review*, 83, 2, pp. 349–371.

Firestone, W. (1998) A Tale of Two Tests: Tensions in Assessment Policy, *Assessment in Education*, 5, 2, pp. 175–191.

Flew, A. (1976) *Sociology, Equality and Education*, London, MacMillan.

Gettier, E. (1963) Is Justified True Belief Knowledge?, *Analysis*, 23, 6, pp. 121–123.

Gipps, C. (1995) *Beyond Testing: Towards a Theory of Educational Assessment*, London, Falmer Press.

Gorard, S. (2006) Value Added Is of Little Value, *Journal of Education Policy*, 21, 2, pp. 235–243.

Goswami, U. (2005) Synthetic Phonics and Learning to Read: A Cross-Language Perspective, *Educational Psychology in Practice*, 21, 4, pp. 273–282.

Gray, J., Goldstein, H. and Jesson, D. (1996) Changes and Improvements in Schools' Effectiveness: Trends over Five Years, *Research Papers in Education*, 11, 1, pp. 35–51.

Harlen, W. (2004) A Systematic Review of the Evidence of Reliability and Validity of Assessment by Teachers Used for Summative Purposes, in *Research Evidence in Education Library (REEL)*, London, EPPE-Centre, Social Science Research Unit, Institute of education.

Harrison, B. (2013) *The Epistemology of Know-How, unpublished PhD thesis, The University of Hertfordshire,* http://hdl.handle.net/2299/10433

HMSO (2008) *Report by the House of Commons, Children, Schools and Families Committee – Testing and Assessment (Session 2007–2008),* London, The Stationery Office Limited.

Hyland, T. (1994) *Competence, Education and NVQs: Dissenting Perpectives,* London, Cassell.

Kripke, S., 1982, *Wittgenstein on Rules and Private Language,* Oxford, Blackwell.

Kuhn, T. (1962) *The Structure of Scientific Revolutions,* Chicago, University of Chicago Press.

Le Grand, J. (2003) *Motivation, Agency and Public Policy,* Oxford, Oxford University Press.

Lum, G. (2012) Two Concepts of Assessment, *Journal of Philosophy of Education,* 46, 4, pp. 589–602.

———. (2013) Competence: A Tale of Two Constructs, *Educational Philosophy and Theory,* 45, 12, pp. 1193–1204.

Mansell, W. (2007) *Education by Numbers: The Tyranny of Testing,* London, Politico's Publishing Ltd.

National Curriculum online (2007) *Attainment Target Level 3,* http://www.nc.uk.net/webdav/harmonise?Page/@id=6001&Session/@id=D_8pdqBGSjXdvEl4aEJkdn&POS[@stateld_eq_main]/@id=6419&POS[@stateld_eq_at]/@id=6419

National Curriculum Task Group on Assessment and Testing (TGAT) (1988) A Report, London, Department of Education and Science.

Nunes, T., Schliemann, A. and Carraher, D. (1993) *Street Mathematics and School Mathematics,* New York, Cambridge University Press.

OECD (2013) *Education at a Glance,* http://www.keepeek.com/Digital-Asset-Management/oecd/education/education-at-a-glance-2013/indicator-a

Ofqual (2011) *A and AS Level Criteria: English Literature,* http://www.ofqual.gov.uk/files/english_lit_perf_des.pdf

Ofsted (1995) *Guidance on the Inspection of Nursery and Primary Schools,* The OFSTED HANDBOOK London, HMSO.

———. (1998a) *The National Numeracy Project: An HMI Evaluation,* London, Office for Standards in Education (OFSTED).

———. (1998b) *Inspection Report on Witton Gilbert Primary School County Durham.*

———. (2003) *Framework 2003 Training: Pre-course Materials for Inspectors: Primary,* http://www.Ofsted.gov.uk/assets/3359.pdf

———. (2004) *The Key Stage 3 Strategy: Evaluation of the Third Year,* Ofsted, London.

———. (2005) *Framework for the Inspection of Schools in England from September 2005,* http://www.Ofsted.gov.uk/publications/2435

————. (2005a) *Cameos – Examples of Best Practice in Teaching*, http://live.ofsted.gov.uk/cameos/index.cfm?fuseaction=search&subjectid=&phaseid=2|Primary&page=13

————. (2005b) *Cameos – Examples of Best Practice in Teaching*, http://live.Ofsted.gov.uk/cameos/index.cfm?fuseaction=search&subjectid=22|Science&phaseid=2|Primary&page=5

————. (2007) *Framework 2005 – Framework for the Inspection of Schools in England from September 2005*, http://www.Ofsted.gov.uk/publications/2435

————. (2014) *Subsidiary Guidance: Supporting the Inspection of Maintained Schools and Academies*, http://www.ofsted.gov.uk/resources/subsidiary-guidance-supporting-inspection-of-maintained-schools-and-academies

Paterson, C. (2013) *Measuring What Matters*, London, Centre Forum.

Paton, G. (2008) *Sats Tests 'Causing Mental Health Problems'*, http://www.telegraph.co.uk/education/3042471/Sats-tests-causing-mental-health-problems.html (last accessed 18 January 2014).

Pring, R. (1992) Standards and Quality in Education, *British Journal of Educational Studies*, XL, 3, pp. 4–22.

QCA (1998) *Standards at Key Stage 2*, London, QCA.

————. (2003) *Foundation Stage Profile Handbook*, https://orderline.qca.org.uk/

————. (2007a) At http://www.nc.uk.net/webdav/harmonise?Page/@id=6001&Session/@id=D_1hBQePcMvRCICCWA4aRl&POS[@stateId_eq_main]/@id=6111&POS[@stateId_eq_note]/@id=6111

————. (2007b) *GCSE Criteria for Applied Art and Design*, http://www.qca.org.uk/qca_4312.aspx#Grade%20descriptions

————. (2007c) *GCSE Criteria for Classical Subjects*, http://www.qca.org.uk/libraryAssets/media/classical_subjects.pdf

————. (2007d) *Subject Criteria for GCSE in Health and Social Care*, http://www.qca.org.uk/qca_6341.aspx#Grade

Rawls, J. (1955) Two Concepts of Rules, *Philosophical Review*, 64, 1, pp. 3–32.

Rosenberg, A. (2011) *Philosophy of Science: A Contemporary Approach* (Third edition), Abingdon, Routledge.

Russell, B. (1912) *The Problems of Philosophy*, Cambridge, The Home University Library

Ruthven, K. (1987) Ability Stereotyping in Mathematics, *Educational Studies in Mathematics*, 18, pp. 243–253.

Ryle, G. (1949) *The Concept of Mind*, London, Hutchinson.

Searle, J. (1995) *The Construction of Social Reality*, London, Penguin Books.

Sternberg, R. (1999) *Cognitive Psychology*, Fort Worth, Harcourt Brace College Publishers.

Stobart, G. (2001) The Validity of National Curriculum Assessment, *British Journal of Educational Studies*, 49, 1, pp. 26–39.

Strauss, V. (2014) *11 Problems Created by the Standardized Testing Obsession*, http://www.washingtonpost.com/blogs/answer-sheet/wp/2014/04/22/11-problems-created-by-the-standardized-testing-obsession/ (last accessed 10 February 2014).

The English National Curriculum (2013) London, HMSO.

The Sutton Trust (2010) http://www.suttontrust.com/news/news/comprehensive-pupils-outperform/ (last accessed 9 March 2014).

Tutt, R. (2012) Lies and Damned Statistics, *Leadership Focus*, 56, p. 15.

Tymms, P. (2004) Are Standards Rising in English Primary Schools?, *British Educational Research Journal*, 30, 4, pp. 477–494.

White, J. P. (1999) Thinking about Assessment, *Journal of Philosophy of Education*, 33, 2, pp. 201–212.

———. (2007) *What Schools Are for and Why. Impact No. 14*, London, Philosophy of Education Society of Great Britain.

Wiliam, D. (2007) Keeping Learning on Track, in F. Lester (ed.) *Second Handbook of Research on Mathematics Teaching and Learning* (volume 2), Charlotte, NC, Information Age Publishing.

Winch, C. and Gingell, J. (1996) Educational Assessment: Reply to Andrew Davis, *Journal of Philosophy of Education*, 30, 3, pp. 337–388.

Index